MOM SPA

75 Relaxing Ways to Pamper a Mother's Mind, Body, and Soul

JENNIFER "GIN" SANDER
Author of *Wear More Cashmere*
and *The Martini Diet*

And the MomSpa Team,
Lindsay Arfsten and Deina Johnson

FAIR WINDS
PRESS
GLOUCESTER, MASSACHUSETTS

Text © 2006 by Jennifer Sander

Illustrations © 2006 by Barbara McGregor/www.artscounselinc.com

A Big City Books Idea

First published in the USA in 2006 by

Fair Winds Press, a member of

Quayside Publishing Group

33 Commercial Street

Gloucester, MA 01930

10 09 08 07 06   1 2 3 4 5

ISBN 1-59233-202-1

Library of Congress Cataloging-in-Publication Data

Sander, Jennifer Basye, 1958-

MomSpa : 75 relaxing ways to pamper a mother's body, mind, and spirit /
Jennifer "Gin" Sander and the MomSpa team, Lindsay Arfsten and Deina Johnson.

p. cm.

"A Big City Books idea."

Includes index.

ISBN 1-59233-202-1

1. Beauty, Personal. 2. Mothers—Health and hygiene. 3. Cosmetics.
4. Relaxation. 5. Pleasure. I. Arfsten, Lindsay. II. Johnson, Deina. III. Title.

RA778.S256 2006

646.7'042--dc22

2005033790

Cover and interior design by Laura McFadden Design, Inc.

laura.mcfadden@rcn.com

Printed and bound in China

The information in this book is for educational purposes only.
It is not intended to replace the advice of a physician or medical practitioner.
Please see your health care provider before beginning any new health program.

ENTS

8   Welcome to MomSpa!

13   75 Relaxing Ways to Pamper a
     Mother's Body, Mind, and Soul

172 Relax, Rejuvenate, Restore – in Minutes!
     Suggestions for Quick Pick-Ups

175 The MomSpa Weekend

180 MomSpa Recipes

192 Beauty and Relaxation Resource Section

INTRO

Mom. Stressed. Those two words could be interchangeable—look up "mom" in the dictionary and find "stressed." Look up "stressed" and find "mom." From sunup to long after sundown, moms everywhere are working hard to keep everyone and everything in their world on an even keel. And as a consequence, sometimes moms feel like they are coming apart themselves. Hmmm...is your life like that too?

We're guessing you might feel that this is an uncanny description of your life, and that's why you now hold this pretty little gift book in your hands. Who are we? Three moms of young kids who've come together as the MomSpa Team in order to help you put some much-needed distance between the words "mom" and "stressed."

In today's world, the word "spa" conjures up images of extreme pampering and indulgence as well as big bucks. Spas are sprouting up like crazy everywhere. As average moms ourselves, we know the average mom doesn't have extra time or money to regularly go in for body-salt glows and hot-rock hydrotherapy massages.

MomSpa is not a book about which "spa treatments" you must try at your local beauty establishment, or a reference for time-consuming, complicated ways to have spa treatments at home. Instead, it focuses on showing you seventy-five easy yet delightful spa-like "ahhh" moments that you can incorporate into your daily life. Husbands and kids can even help create a spa feeling at home by planning to let you sleep in, bringing you your morning cup of coffee and the paper, and then fixing breakfast on their own to give you more peace-and-quiet time. Why should we wait for our once-a-year Mother's Day pampering?

Do mothers deserve the extra attention, time for ourselves, and luxury of a few special things to bring us soothing joy in our lives? *Yes!*

Moms do seem to have some reluctance about making time for or spending money on themselves. Think of it this way: If you feel healthier, happier, or simply mellower, won't you pass that feeling on to your loved ones?

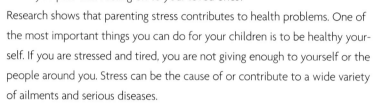

Research shows that parenting stress contributes to health problems. One of the most important things you can do for your children is to be healthy yourself. If you are stressed and tired, you are not giving enough to yourself or the people around you. Stress can be the cause of or contribute to a wide variety of ailments and serious diseases.

Skip the guilt when it comes to taking care of yourself, to pampering and treating yourself well. Yes, we know that is a hard philosophy for some women to adopt, but mothers need to make it a priority to carve out time for relaxation whenever we can. We should regularly do the things that give us peace and serenity in our daily lives, which includes turning off the noise and busyness that so often fill up our heads and directs our bodies. Unless we are regularly taking care of ourselves, our bodies and our minds are in danger of simply burning out.

Our children need for us to be there for them wholly and completely. But *we* need to be whole and complete in order to take good care of them. We need to be healthy and happy first before we can have healthy, happy children. It's difficult to teach our children how to be healthy and happy without modeling it ourselves. We can't depend on anyone else to make us healthy. Doctors help us when we're sick, but true preventative health must come from our thoughts and actions. This is our responsibility to ourselves and our families. True health means to be sound and vibrantly well on all levels of being: physical, emotional, mental, and spiritual.

Our book is bursting with ideas to add joy, bliss, laughs, peace, vibrancy, health, and love to your life. Take a deep breath in, hold, and slowly exhale. And now, dive in!

MEET THE MOMSPA TEAM

Jennifer: The mother of two grade-school boys, Julian and Jonathan. Between packing lunches and picking up stray skateboards, Jennifer works hard at keeping her own needs on her "to-do" list. The author of the book *Wear More Cashmere*, she is "America's Affordable Luxury Expert" and has developed countless small ways to help mothers feel indulged and pampered in the midst of a hectic day.

Lindsay: The mother of three young daughters, Sara, Carly, and Julia (each just one scant year apart!), Lindsay grabs quiet moments wherever she can. Between the kids and her home-based business, Lindsay is on the go constantly. A certified yoga instructor, she has developed techniques we can all use to achieve inner quiet and calm.

Deina: The mother of toddlers Max and Delaney, Deina has spent twenty years in the beauty business as a day spa owner and licensed aesthetician. She knows all the professional tricks of the trade and has developed easy and inexpensive ways for any mom to have a spa experience at home.

Three different women, three different lives, three different approaches to feeling pampered. Jennifer could fill your day with seventy-five ways to feel girly, Lindsay could give you seventy-five ways to feel reinvigorated, and Deina could easily give you seventy-five ways to keep your brow smooth and your eyes bright.

But we realized it will be more useful to you and your needs to pool our methods and ideas into more of a mixed spa bag. There will be days in your life when the MomSpa experience you really need is a long, quiet soak in an herb-infused bath. Or perhaps a stressful moment with your kids in the midst of the grocery store will require one of Lindsay's breathing exercises and a silent chant (Jennifer's chant is "Starbucks, Starbucks, Starbucks") to get you safely out the door. Should a day arise when your whole brood is gone for more than an hour or two, you can plan the afternoon around one of Deina's indulgent beauty treatments. You'll find ideas for every mood and occasion.

WHAT'S INSIDE

As we've said, in *MomSpa* you'll find seventy-five deliciously relaxing ways to pamper yourself. But that's not all! Mixed in throughout are ways that you and your husband or partner can share the pampering experience. Remember the wise biblical advice to "Do unto others..."? Try these techniques, and you'll find that your husband or partner will soon do unto you! We've also highlighted fun ways that mothers and daughters can share in some of these pampering treats too. Lindsay has passed many a delightful afternoon with her little girls beautifying and pampering each other.

We know how pressed for time you can be, so we have included a helpful section that will give you ideas on what you can do now, right away, should you have an extra fifteen minutes, a surprise free hour, or a blissful day to yourself.

And what is a spa without spa food? For those days when you can give yourself the ultimate gift of cooking for your own tastes instead of what everyone else wants (steak, peanut butter and jelly, macaroni and cheese...), we've supplied our own favorite light meals to pamper and delight your palate.

A family budget can easily get stretched too tightly, and we always keep that in mind when designing our MomSpa moments. Some of our creations involve clever ways to use what you already have around the house—the humidifier in your children's room, for instance, or the rice cooker you haven't used in years—and put it to use in a different way. You'll soon learn that some of the best ways to feel pampered are actually free! We've listed great sources for ingredients in the back of the book, but much of what you need—dried herbs and essential oils—can be found at your local health food store or in a big grocery store.

Are you ready to relax? Are you ready to pamper yourself and indulge in ways big and small? Come on then, you *spa*, girl!

75

RELAXING WAYS TO PAMPER A MOTHER'S BODY, MIND, AND SOUL

IT WAS ONE OF THOSE DAYS. One of those Mondays when nothing is going right and shouting loudly at everyone seems to be the only option. Here is another option, a MomSpa alternative to making a scene or drinking the cooking sherry.

LEMON LAVENDER LIFT

TREAT YOUR FEET TO A LEMON LAVENDER LIFT. IN JUST 30 MINUTES, you will have feet that are baby-bottom-smooth—and you'll feel calmer from the soothing scent of fresh lavender, so you'll no longer feel the need to shout at anyone.

Having your feet massaged is heavenly. There are many pressure points in your feet that, when pressed and massaged, will help your body to release tension and stress and eliminate toxins.

What You'll Need

Lemon Lavender Lift Foot Rub

¼ cup (75 g) Epsom salts

½ cup (150 g) sea salt

2 ounces (60 ml) apricot kernel oil

10 drops lemon essential oil

20 drops lavender essential oil

2 tablespoons chopped lemon zest

3 dried lavender buds, seeds removed from twigs

You'll also need a glass bowl for the scrub, a plastic tub large enough to soak both of your feet at once, a large fluffy towel, and a roll of plastic wrap.

Mix all of the ingredients in a glass bowl. Sit down in a comfortable low chair and soak your feet in a plastic tub filled with warm water for about 10 minutes. Dry with the towel, and then place the towel on the floor under your feet. Dip your fingers into the mixture and take a small scoop, just enough to rub a small section. You don't want to end up with too much of the scrub in your hand at one time. Working on small areas, give yourself a thorough foot massage with the mixture. Be sure to concentrate on your heels and other rough patches.

If you have an extra half-hour to spare, wrap plastic wrap around your feet and tuck them into the towel. Your own body temperature will create a mini heater that will allow the oils to soak in even further.

After you've rubbed both of your feet into smoothness (or when your children just won't leave you alone any longer), rinse your feet in the plastic tub and pat dry. Now is the perfect time to apply a heavy lotion to help retain the smoothness.

See how easy it was to create your own custom beauty product? Once you learn how to mix a simple scrub like this, you can begin to experiment with all kinds of other ingredients. Do you have an herb garden handy? Start picking leaves and crushing them in your hands to see what kinds of scents and mixtures you can develop. Rosemary is wonderful, and so is mint. You might develop combinations that address different moods and situations: an earthy, woodsy scent to use with your partner as a romantic get-in-the-mood gesture, or a sweetly perfumed scent for days when you have the house to yourself. Use your imagination and see what you can come up with!

Reflexology 101

Reflexology is based on the idea that areas on your feet correspond to other areas throughout your body. So, if you rub or massage a specific part of your foot, not only will your foot feel better, but so will the corresponding body part! Here's what you need to know about reflexology to give a great foot massage: When rubbing the ankle area, you are connected to your body's reproductive area. Reach down and feel the base of your heel—this whole area is related to the back bone. When you rub the bottom of the foot, you are hitting the adrenal areas to detox the body. Reflexology works to release negative energy, too. The areas in between the toes are related to the sinuses, eyes, ears, nose, and the facial area, and the base of the big toe is related to the base of the neck. Next time you give (or get) a foot rub, try it and see what you think!

LiNDSay waS SuRPRiSED WhEN yoᴳa ENTERED hER,LiFE. There she was, pounding away at the Stairmaster in the local gym, when the yoga instructor approached her. "No one showed up for my class today, would you like to try?" "No!" was what Lindsay thought to herself, preferring to focus on burning calories in what little spare time she had. But being a nice gal, she smiled and agreed.

"I was prepared for some easy, old lady, boring class and was already planning an extra workout that week to make up for lost Stairmaster time," says Lindsay. "After all, I was trying to burn off multi-pregnancy weight gains. But much to my surprise, I loved moving my body in new ways. If you haven't tried yoga, the only way I can describe the feeling is like the relaxation achieved in a full-body massage."

Lindsay has since gone on to study yoga and become a certified instructor. Here is one of her favorite anywhere/anytime stretches.

SHOULDER DROPS AND NECK ROLLS

SHOULDER DROPS AND NECK ROLLS ARE IDEAL FOR THOSE moments when you need to do something for yourself, but have only a minute to spare. So in that minute, sit on the floor. Go ahead, just sit down wherever you find yourself—you need this!

While simply sitting on the floor with your legs crossed, purposely drop your shoulders. Let them relax and drop several inches—you've been holding them up all day. Allow your chin to drop to your chest as you take deep breaths. Dropping your chin down will help you lower your shoulders even further, to release all of that pent-up tension and stress.

Now work your neck into it. Start with your chin down on your chest and begin to slowly, very slowly, move your head around in a roll. Listen to those creaky muscles and joints as you move around! Doesn't it feel great? Try to do at least five rolls in one direction, and five in the other, before you have to stand up and go about your life again. When your time is up, don't just jump up. Instead, give yourself the time to stretch and stand slowly.

MiDDay STRETCh

Jennifer's favorite middle-of-the-day stretch is to stand in the doorway between rooms and reach up for the doorjamb. Try to stretch your fingers to touch it, and if you are tall enough, try to grab on a tiny bit and at the same time lower your heels back towards the floor. A wonderful stretch for your back!

SCENTED STEAM

3

Something that doesn't involve leaving a candle lit around small children? Something so that, instead of living in a house that smells of gym socks and peanut butter more often than not, you can move through rooms that smell more like an elegant hotel?

Deina came up with a wonderful new use for the vaporizer or humidifier every mom has hanging around for when the kids get a cold. She uses hers throughout the winter with essential oils and loose herbs added to the water in order to give the moist air a hint of scent and to help her family fight the yearly colds.

"I prepare my vaporizer starting in the month of November," Deina explains. "I take down my children's old vaporizer and fill it with water, then add oils to discourage the spread of colds and unwanted germs. It really works for me and my family! Eucalyptus, rosemary, and lemon are great antibacterial herbs that relieve the symptoms of colds. Try it!"

20

ADDING A LITTLE SOMETHING TO A VAPORIZER OR HUMIDIFIER IS EASY.
Follow the directions on your appliance for how much water to add,
and then simply shake in a handful of crushed fresh herbs like lavender or rosemary. Jennifer fills her humidifier with water and then
taps in 20 drops of lavender oil. Plug it in, and when the steam
begins to emerge, it will fill the air with a pleasant cloud of lavender.

Hot Herbal Compress

For another great pick-me-up, you can make a hot herbal compress. Toss a handful
of healing herbs such as peppermint, chamomile, or lavender into a saucepan full of
water and allow them to come to a boil. Turn off the heat and let the herbs steep
for a few minutes. Strain out the herbs, and then soak a washcloth in the warm
brew. Twist out the excess water, find a relaxing place to recline for a few minutes,
and place the warm compress gently on your face. Be careful not to put it on your
face when it is still hot to the touch! Breathe deeply and enjoy the moment.

If you are reluctant to add a little something extra to the water
itself, you could also put the essential oil on a cotton ball and
place it near the steam vent on your machine. Some machines
have a receptacle into which medication can be added. Place the
oil-soaked cotton ball in this area if yours has one.

Wonderful Washcloth Trick

Another great spa use for an appliance you might already own is to warm towels in
your rice cooker. Think of those little hot towels you used to get on long flights or at
Asian restaurants to wash your hands and face. They are wonderful to add to a foot-
scrub routine. (See page 15 for Lemon Lavender Lift foot rub.) Fill a small bowl with
water and add a few drops of your favorite oil essence. Mix the scent, and then wet
a washcloth in the scented water. Wring it out and fold it carefully. Place it inside a
clean rice cooker and let it steam for five minutes. Remove with tongs (just the way
the flight attendant does!) and apply carefully. Don't put it against your face until it
is cool enough to handle; Be very cautious, please.

"THE THOUGHT OF ROMANCE ALWAYS SEEMS GREAT, but by the time my husband and I have time just for each other, we are exhausted," says Deina. "One way to try to keep the romance alive is with a little help from aromatherapy."

ROMANCE IN THE AIR

4

AFTER A LONG DAY OF CHASING KIDS, IT'S ALL TOO easy to focus more on how wonderful it will feel to sleep than on how wonderful it will feel to lie in your husband's arms. The slightly scented aroma of your bedroom will serve as a subtle reminder that romance is a critical part of the MomSpa approach to living.

Now that you know how to use your vaporizer or humidifier to add a little extra scent to your rooms, why not bring it into the bedroom? Deina relies on the scent of jasmine, vanilla, or sandalwood to encourage closeness. Those earthy yet soothing smells (particularly vanilla) can work wonders on a man.

As described in Scented Steam (see page 20), Deina uses her children's vaporizer and adds herbs and essential oils to the water.

MomSpa Magic

Jennifer is addicted to the free perfume samples that come in every magazine nowadays. She rips the page out of the magazine, tears off the perfumed section, opens it up, and slips it between her sheets when she makes the bed in the morning to add a delicate scent. Try to remember to remove the sample at night, though: no one wants to turn over onto a crunchy piece of paper!

Another way to develop a romantic air in your bedroom is with fragrant sachets. Deina makes them from cotton squares.

What you'll Need

Herbal Sachets

2 tablespoons dried herbs

2 cotton squares (3 inches, or 7.5 cm, each)

Place the dried herbs in the center of one square. Cover with the other square and use your best basting stitch to enclose the edges. Don't worry if your sewing skills are rough—no one will see these little sachets as you slip them inside your pillowcase.

Ah, you hear the car door slam and the sound of the car pulling out of the driveway. Your husband and the kids have just headed out for a few hours, and the house is yours! Time for an instant getaway, one you have planned for. Because you've already prepared everything you need, you're ready to swing into instant action. The beauty of this "instant getaway" is that you really aren't going anywhere. You are staying at home, in your own house, but for a few precious hours you can be mentally far away...

INSTANT GETAWAY 5

MomSpa Magic

Jennifer's robe is from her favorite California spa at the Half Moon Bay Ritz-Carlton. Perhaps you can buy a thick robe from your favorite hotel, spa, or getaway. For these special alone-times, don't put on your everyday robe! It really is a great feeling to have purchased a special robe for these kinds of events. Slipping into that special robe puts you right into the pampering mood. Okay, perhaps you can also take it on romantic vacations with your husband, but do make it a point to keep one lounging-around outfit that is only for the moments when you are treating yourself, and not for the days when you are wandering around the house picking up stray socks and soggy dog toys.

JENNIFER BOUGHT A LARGE OVERNIGHT BAG AT AN OUTLET MALL WITH these very occasions in mind. Not that she was going to go anywhere with it, mind you, but a girl can always dream! Here's what she keeps in a small suitcase in the back of the closet at all times and pulls out whenever she has the chance to relax alone at home for a few hours:

What you'll Need

Instant Getaway Suitcase
A plush terry robe
Luxury shampoo and conditioner, not the everyday stuff
Wooden massage roller
Lavender spa booties
A favorite CD (hers is Les Nubians, a sexy French duo)
Luxury lotions like Thymes Goldleaf

Pack your own suitcase now with all of your favorite ready-to-use items (this is no time to be whipping up your own treatments). Keep it close at hand so that when the opportunity arises, you can seize the moment, or the hour, or—blissful thought—the entire day.

DIY Back Massage

Even if your family has just run down to the store for a quick trip, you can still fit in a do-it-yourself back massage. All you need are a few tennis balls! Lie down on a yoga mat or on your own carpeted floor and place the balls on either side of your spine at the base of your back. Relax and let your weight settle on the balls (we admit, it *is* a strange feeling). Once you are accustomed to the feeling, begin to move yourself up and down a bit so that the balls move across your tense muscles. It sounds wacky, but it feels wonderful. Give it a try!

WE CAN ALL GET SO BOGGED DOWN IN OUR OWN LIVES AND WHAT IS HAPPENING TO US THAT WE FAIL TO SEE IT ALL FROM A LARGER PERSPECTIVE. Do you ever have those days when you focus on something negative—maybe the fact that you hate the wallpaper in your bedroom—and that negative thought soon drags the rest of your day down? If you change your perspective in the middle of your pity party, you will feel better, lighter, and even thankful.

Lindsay knows this well. While wallowing in self-pity over a crop of hormonal zits on her chin, she ran into a friend who was also struggling, but with a major medical condition instead of a temporary and superficial annoyance. Instant perspective change.

Even with this newfound understanding, Lindsay allowed herself to wallow in the fact that her bedroom furniture was out of date.

Just as Lindsay's lip began to pout outwards, along came the day's mail with a brochure from Habitat for Humanity. These wonderful folks build houses for the needy all over the world, and the brochure highlighted efforts to rebuild after the horrific floods in New Orleans and the tsunami in Southeast Asia. "How could I be engaged in an 'I don't have a nice bedroom set' pity party when thousands of families had literally nothing at all?" Lindsay asked herself.

A CHANGE IN PERSPECTIVE

FEELING DOWN ABOUT MONEY, YOUR LOOKS, YOUR RELATIONSHIPS, OR other things is usually a matter of perspective. Use the MomSpa method to change your thought process: Turn an "I wish…" statement into an "I'm so thankful for…" statement. Just focus on flipping that switch—it's really that easy. Anytime you need to de-stress or change your perspective from one of pity to one of plenty, just run through all of the things you have to be thankful for in your mind, say them out loud, or write them down. Pity? Forget it! When you think of all of the true riches in your life, you'll feel ready to party!

What is it that you are negatively focused on in your life right now? Kids? Money? Lousy furniture? Your children might be undoing all the hard work you've done cleaning the house, but remember: They are healthy and strong enough to make a mess. Money can easily consume all of our thoughts, but we must not let it. Life, love, health, and happiness are what matter—money's just a tool. And as for your furniture, hey, take an upholstery course, learn a useful skill, and gain the satisfaction of doing it all yourself!

FEEL BAD? DO GOOD!

The next time you find yourself drawn into self-pity, step back and think, "How can I do the most good with this feeling?" If you are unhappy with your looks, why not send off a charitable donation to an organization that helps children born with cleft palates? Feeling disappointed that your family vacation will be too short this year? Send a small donation to a community group that takes inner city kids to camp. And yes, when you are annoyed that your interior decoration looks dated, look for a Habitat for Humanity project near you and get involved (www.habitatforhumanity.org)!

Ahhh, Asia. Thoughts and images of Asia are almost always so restful by their very nature. Everything just seems so much more peaceful in that part of the world. Orderly. Balanced. Calm. Exotic. When all is in chaos around Jennifer's house, she often closes her eyes and thinks of a favorite spa in Tokyo. Jumping on a jet is not a reasonable option, so instead she seeks out a little Oriental calm nearby.

JAPANESE RETREAT

ONE OF THE GREAT GIFTS OF THE ORIENT IS GREEN TEA. GREEN TEA is rich in antioxidants, which help slow the aging process. So fight of Father Time with a hot cup morning and evening! If the taste of plain green tea is too bland for your liking, add some fresh-squeezed lemon or lime juice and honey (also rich in nutrients and antioxidants) to boost the taste.

Don't limit yourself to drinking green tea, though. Try these easy, wonderful beauty secrets. Start by brewing some green tea, then chill the tea in the fridge. Use the ice-cold brew to refresh and restore tired, sore skin.

Here are some suggestions:

1. Dip cottonballs in the cold tea and press on closed eyelids to refresh tired eyes.
2. Dab the tea on your face or use as a rinse to fight acne.
3. Soothe sunburned skin by dabbing on the cold tea.
4. Soak tired, sore feet in a basin of icy green tea.

WONDERFUL JAPANESE BEAUTY PRODUCTS

The most well-known Japanese beauty company is Shiseido, but a new company has recently emerged that now makes products that are available in the United States. DHC is a large skin-care company founded in Japan some twenty years ago that bases their products on a rather un-Japanese ingredient: olive oil. All of their lotions and cleansers are based on organic olive oil, which is rich in vitamins and antioxidants. What Jennifer loves most about them is that their catalog comes stuffed with tiny free samples of their products! To request a catalog, visit their Web site at www.dhccare.com.

KITCHEN QUICKIES

How many hours do we all spend in our kitchens? The number would be depressingly high, so let's just skip it. But hey, as long as we're there, what can we be doing for ourselves at the same time we're working to feed our families or to clean up after feeding our families?

DEINA TAKES THE OPPORTUNITY TO LIGHTLY STEAM HER FACE WHEN cooking on the stove. Do be careful, of course, as a big blast of hot steam can easily burn you. As long as you are at the stove in charge of a pan or two, you could put on an extra small pan of water with herbs added to steam at a more controllable temperature.

Here are some more fast and easy ideas:

Rub a tiny bit of olive oil into the ends of your hair while working around the kitchen. Don't use so much that your hair looks gloppy and unwashed for the rest of the evening; use just a teensy amount on the ends to give them a moisture boost. If you can leave the olive oil in overnight and wash your hair the following morning, you will have had quite a lengthy beauty treatment!

You can also rub small amounts of olive oil gently into the skin on the backs of your hands to add moisture to the delicate areas there. Leave your fingers oil-free, but let the rich olive oil sink into the thin skin of your hands for a more youthful look.

Another simple hand treatment is to use lemon juice on the age spots on the backs of your hands. Squeeze lemon juice into a small cup and add a drop or two of water. Dip your fingers into the mixture and then pat it onto your brown spots. Let the mixture dry, and leave it on for another twenty minutes or so before rinsing your hands.

Spa Secrets

Remember, almost all beauty treatments started in the kitchen. Famous face creams were developed over stoves by Estée Lauder and Helena Rubinstein. Anita Roddick of the Body Shop used homely and basic ingredients like oatmeal in her first products. So don't be shy about trying what you have lying around in the kitchen, too. Think citrus to tone, oils to moisturize, and don't forget the lowly egg white as a famous skin tightener! Get creative and make something up. Who knows—it might lead you to start your own beauty empire!

LIFE WOULD BE A DREAM if we all had the time and the money to head for a spa anytime we needed it. Sadly, family responsibilities and the size of the bank balance all too often interfere. Here is a quick way to get a small dose of that spa-good-feeling—take care of your car!

CAN'T TREAT YOURSELF? TREAT YOUR CAR!

9

YES, WE KNOW HOW BADLY YOU ARE IN need of a body buff, polish on your nails, and a relaxing steam-cleaning. But that can take hours of time and hundreds of dollars. For a quick lift, you can just pull into the car wash and get those very things done to your car! A clean and orderly house can sometimes give you the mental lift you need (an even bigger lift if someone else has cleaned it for you!), right? The same goes for your poor, trashed car.

Keeping your car clean and sweet-smelling will go a long way toward turning your daily commute into a relaxing retreat. But don't stop there. Choose a selection of relaxing CDs to listen to on the way to and from work. (This is not the time to tune into the news with its daily horrors, or hard rock, which studies show makes people drive too fast!) Pack a mini-spa in a makeup bag and keep it in your car. It will come in handy while you're sitting in the parking lot waiting for the kids. Make sure yours has tissues, hand lotion, your favorite essential oils for dabbing, and a beloved lipstick. A pack of refreshing breath mints never hurts, either!

Once your car has been given the once-over, break out one of those perfume strips from your latest magazine and stick it in the door pocket. You can drive a gleaming car and smell a high-end scent at the same time!

SOUNDS A BIT LIKE A HIGH SCHOOL ESSAY ASSIGNMENT, DOESN'T IT? "Ten Things You Love, and Why You Love Them." No, we don't mean to add homework to your already busy day, but we do want you to sit and think hard about just which ten things you do love. So pour a cup of this morning's leftover coffee and start making your list.

TEN THINGS YOU LOVE

LET YOURSELF BE PERFECTLY FRANK AND FREE ABOUT WHAT YOU WRITE down: Don't be embarrassed or shy or shocked by what you come up with (because we wouldn't be!)—this is not a list you need to share with anyone else.

What is the point, then? The point is this: Once you come up with the list of ten things you love, try to make sure that, each and every day of your life, you are doing at least two of them! More is better, but two is the bare minimum.

A list might include kissing, hugging, listening to music, hanging out with your family, dancing, snuggling (or whatever you want to call it!), working in your garden, reading a book, eating pizza, eating chocolate, eating ice cream, eating...oh, you get the point. Write your list on a piece of nice paper, perhaps design it on your computer to add a professional air, and then carry it around with you at all times.

Having a bad, stressful day? Pull out your list and see which of the things you love you could do *right that minute*. Love dancing? Maybe a quick samba step in the grocery store aisle is all you will need to perk yourself up. Passionate about gardening? Maybe a five-minute weed-pulling session outdoors in your garden will help you blow off steam. If your garden isn't close at hand, perhaps you could just focus quietly on a vase of flowers in your office, or gaze out the window at a neatly tended patch of green grass.

This sounds like such a simple idea, and it is. But we all too often overlook the things we love and focus on all that is unpleasant around us. Stop. Breathe. Do something you love. Better yet, do two or three.

IF YOU ARE EASILY SHOCKED, please skip to the next MomSpa idea. If, on the other hand, you are a mature woman involved in a healthy and loving sexual relationship, and if you have gone through the birth process once or twice or more, we doubt you will be too surprised by what we have to say.

THE SECRET SQUEEZE

11

OKAY, HERE IT IS: ONE OF JENNIFER'S FAVORITE SECRETLY INDULGENT MomSpa activities is...Kegeling. Kegeling? Is that like yodeling? No, it means doing Kegels. Yes, Kegels, those exercises your doctor told you to do before and after your babies were born. Those exercises that every sex manual recommends in order to strengthen the very muscles used in lovemaking...*those* Kegels.

Kegels involve working your pubococcygeus muscles, also known as PC muscles. Now, if you know how to Kegel, then Kegel away, particularly at times when no one can guess what you are up to. Kegel while you're at stop signs, Kegel while you're in line for bagels, Kegel while you're surfing online... keep those muscles strong and tight!

If you don't know how or what, then listen up: The next time you use the toilet, stop your urine in midstream. Easy, isn't it? Well, you just found your PC muscles. Now that you've located them, you can give them a workout any time of the day, no bathroom required. Squeeze and hold for several seconds in sets of ten. Start off with just a few gentle sets a day of these secret squeezes, and work up to more often and a stronger squeeze.

The next time you can't get to the gym, don't feel too bad. Go ahead and do some secret exercises and work out that special part of your body.

Turn off the Tap

Age and childbirth can both have the same effect: A little incontinence can occur at times. The cure to stop that annoying and embarrassing problem? You guessed it, Kegels. A regular routine can strengthen the urinary muscles.

DREaMING OF SOMEDaY BEING THE MISTRESS OF a SUMPTUOUS aND BOUNTIFUL FLOWER GaRDEN in which you can walk alone for hours on end? Hey, so are we! Alas, sumptuousness and bounty are still on the to-do list—maybe we'll get around to them after we all get done paying college tuition bills some decade in the future.

STOP AND SMELL SOMEONE ELSE'S ROSES

IF YOU, TOO, ARE GARDENLESS, DON'T DESPAIR. THE PEACE AND CALM that comes from spending time in a garden can still be yours, but you will have to borrow the garden from someone else.

Almost every town has a great public garden, and almost all of them are underused. Seek out the quiet calm of a garden in the early afternoon, and don't be surprised to find that you can wander alone and imagine it really is your very own. Bring along a sandwich and a thermos of tea and choose a favorite bench to sit on during each visit.

If you can't find a public garden in your town, go ahead and ask a friend if you can borrow hers. Gardeners love to share, and any garden-owning friend will certainly be honored if you ask for a visit. Be bold: Go ahead and confess that you are on the hunt for a quiet and restful place to sit and read a book.

Of course, this works best on a kid-free outing on your own. There is nothing restful about spending time worrying that Junior might yank out someone's prize roses or that Baby might crawl into a patch of poison oak or ivy!

FINDING GREAT GARDENS

There are great public gardens scattered around the country, and you could plan an amazing vacation around them. Check out the Krohn Conservatory in Cincinnati, Ohio; the world-famous rose gardens in Tyler, Texas; Longwood Gardens in Kennett Square, Pennsylvania; and the big botanical gardens in New York, San Francisco, and in Norfolk, Virginia.

WhaT couLD BE moRE hEaVENLy ThaN a LoNG aND LEiSURELy SoaK, iN a hoT TUB? Perhaps one in which you were surrounded by the soothing scent of herbs, while your skin soaked up the natural healing properties of the herbs and your mind was left to wander far afield...

THE HERBAL BATH

13

ONE OF DEINA'S FAVORITE THINGS TO DO IS TO TAKE A BATH AT NIGHT after the children are in bed. It might be only a 10-minute bath, or it might be a 45-minute bath; she enjoys whatever she can get.

She adds herbs like lavender, jasmine, or rosemary to her bath, herbs that are easy to find in a health food store. Either sprinkle the loose herbs on the water (and rinse them off when you are done) or tuck the herbs in muslin bath bags, also sold in health food stores.

Deina runs a tub full of very hot water, adds the herbs, and then lets them steep for 30 minutes while she reads her children a bedtime story. If she doesn't have the time to steep herbs in the tub, she boils a pot of water on the stove, adds the herbs, allows them to steep for 15 minutes, and then adds the water to a bath.

"I love rubbing my body with the muslin bag to feel the concentrated herbs," Deina confesses, and you will too, once you learn to make this easy herbal bath treat.

What You'll Need

¼ cup dried lavender, rosemary, jasmine, or other herbs

Add the dried herbs to hot water and allow to steep for at least 15 minutes before entering your bath.

As you read through this Book,

you will discover many different delightful indulgences you just can't wait to try on your own. Better yet, why not share your newfound knowledge with a few girlfriends and have your own spa party to celebrate the MomSpa philosophy?

SPA PARTY!

14

ROUND UP A FEW OTHER STRESSED-OUT MOMS ON A NIGHT WHEN EVERYONE has child care (sorry, no children allowed, as the point of this evening is to relax completely). Set the stage for your friends with scented candles and sweet-smelling incense, or put a pot of water with fragrant herbs like rosemary or lavender on the stove to simmer all night long.

What kinds of treatments could you do at your home MomSpa party? Why not get everyone involved in a heavenly foot treatment like the Lemon Lavender Lift (see page 15), followed by foot massages for each other? Follow the treatment with herbal compresses (see page 21) and a do-it-yourself one-minute manicure scrub and lotion, and you will all feel like supreme queens.

Party Profits

What fun to have a bunch of friends over for a party! And it's even more fun if you can make an extra dollar or two! There are several companies that now specialize in party-plan businesses with a focus on spa treatments and beauty. Beauty Control is the largest, owned by the same folks who do Tupperware. Adora is an up-and-coming entrant into the field, if you prefer to work with a smaller company. Check out their Web site at www.adoraspa.com.

You can't have a party without food, now, can you? At a spa party, you should stay away from the gloppy and heavy traditional party foods like chips and dips. Instead, set out plates of sliced fresh fruits and vegetables, yogurt dips, and nutritious smoothies. There is a whole spa-food recipe chapter at the end of this book to help you with ideas. (It begins on page 180.)

Before you invite your friends, make sure you have these essentials on hand:

- Enough plastic tubs to soak everyone's feet (easy to find at a dollar store)
- Enough thick towels so that everyone gets two of their own (they will need them both!)
- A few hand mirrors (so you can pass them around for a good giggle once the masks go on!)
- Small bowls and spoons for individual treatments

End the evening with breathing exercises (see page 000) so that your guests learn a stress-reduction technique they can rely on in the future.

FEELING THE NEED TO DO SOMETHING FOR YOURSELF, BUT TOTALLY SHORT ON TIME?
Employ Jennifer's favorite technique for a quick beauty treatment—tooth-whitening strips! Sometimes a facial is too messy, a massage is too long, a manicure is too wet, and meditation is *toooo slooowww*. But putting whitening strips in your mouth and going on about the rest of your business for half an hour is just right.

15

WHAT BRIGHT, WHITE TEETH YOU HAVE!

OVER-THE-COUNTER TOOTH-WHITENING products are very reasonably priced. Generics now run in the $20 range, and even the higher-priced products are still an affordable $30 or so. Jennifer is fond of the Crest Whitestrips Premium, which have given her very good results in the past (and saved her several hundred dollars at the dentist's office).

And here is the big MomSpa bonus: She claims her method not only results in brighter teeth, but also higher cheekbones. Oh, really? Yes, in her book *The Martini Diet: The Self-Indulgent Way to a Thinner, More Fabulous You,* Jennifer offered up a number of "Cinnabon-avoidance techniques" (that is, ways to prevent snacking.) One of the best is to pop in a tooth-whitening strip whenever you have a weak moment and feel a potato chip binge coming on, or hear a tub of ice cream calling to you from the freezer late at night. (You know those moments, don't you?) Why does this work? Well, who wants to eat ice cream—or even a Cinnabon—when her mouth is tingling with a blast of mint?

TEas FOR.YouR. TEETh

Wake up your mouth and freshen your breath with a cup of peppermint tea. (Peppermint tea also improves poor digestion, a frequent cause of bad breath.) Try some chamomile tea to soothe sore gums. Here's another trick! Brew up a cup of thyme tea using 2 teaspoons dried thyme. Steep 5 minutes, then dip your dental floss in the tea before flossing to soothe your gums and keep your whole mouth feeling good.

16

CATCH A CATNAP

SLEEP: SOMETHING WE MOMS NEVER SEEM TO GET ENOUGH OF. Between late nights spent straightening the house after everyone else is in bed and middle-of-the-night awakenings by small children seeking comfort, a good night's rest seems all too elusive. So maybe you just need to get it during the daytime! "I nap daily," Judith Horstman, an alternative health writer, told us, "That is my number-one indulgence." Judith claims she learned "The Art of the Nap" in drama school, and has practiced it in 20-minute segments ever since. "Even when my children were little, I would gather them all in my bed, give them picture books, and tell them to stay right there while mommy took a tiny nap. It made them feel very important to be in charge while I slept next to them for a short while."

HERE IS JUDITH'S ADVICE ON HOW to fall asleep in 60 seconds:

"I lie back on the sofa with one of those lovely silk eye pillows, put it in place, and immediately start to count backwards from 100," she says. "I count very, very slowly, while concentrating on my breathing. Become aware of your breathing as a meditative focus; it helps you shut your mind off of other things. I also focus on the idea of 'black on black,' in that I conjure up a mental picture of absolutely nothing."

To take a short nap, you might at first need to have an alarm clock to wake you. If you make short naps a habit, however, your body will soon learn to go into a deep sleep and then emerge in the proper amount of time.

MomSpa Magic

A little silk eye pillow does sound divine, but what if you don't have one on hand? A dark-colored washcloth can easily do the trick, folded into thirds and draped across your eyes. To add a bit of aromatherapy relaxation to the mix, you can wet a bit of the cloth and then tap a few drops—three or four—of essential oils onto the damp part. Fold the cloth so that the damp part is on top, away from your skin, and then lie back with it over your eyes. Take deep breaths and enjoy the scent. Jennifer likes to use lavender to help induce an easy sleep. When indulging in this scented relaxation technique, take care never to get any essential oil in your eyes.

Don't Skip Sleep!

Never overlook how important sleep is to your overall health and happiness. You are a busy woman, but your body still requires at least seven hours of sleep a night; otherwise, you'll slip into sleep deprivation. A full 68 percent of American women report being sleep-deprived. Developing the quick catnap habit can help you stay out of that camp.

LiNDSay BELiEVES ThaT haRBoRiNG DEEP RESENTmENT TOWaRDS SomEONE ROBS yoUR, SoUL oF TOTaL Joy. "It's not good for our health, it does not set a good example for our kids, it is a sin, and it blocks our soul from true happiness," she says. "I've struggled with it in my own life, particularly with my mother. And I know it is easier to say 'I forgive you' than it is to really feel it in your heart."

LEARN TO FORGIVE

LEARNING TO FORGIVE? WHY ARE WE INCLUDING THIS IN *MOMSPA*? Because we want you to take care of *all* parts of yourself—from your skin to your psyche, from your mouth to your mood. Our bodies and our hearts are intertwined, and for us to truly be rested, relaxed, and yes, pampered, we must be at peace. Will you really benefit from a massage if all you do is lie there and obsess on a wrong someone has done you? Will you truly gain from a yoga stretch if your body is kinked because you are angry with someone? Here are several ways Lindsay recommends we learn to forgive those we believe have wronged us (or our families).

"If you need to forgive someone who isn't there, go ahead and write it all out in a letter. Pour it all out on the page as openly and honestly as possible. Once you've expelled all that negativity from your soul and onto the paper, tear it up and move on.

Another technique that Lindsay practices is to sit cross-legged on the floor in a quiet, undisturbed place. "Envision yourself sitting at the bottom of a warm, clear lake," she says. "You are enveloped by the water and feel the gentle movement around you. You look up and see rays of sunshine coming down through the water. Let the sunlight and the warm lapping water soothe and relax you. Feel the tension draining away as the water gently caresses you." Once you can visualize this meditation and feel the sensation you can use itot rebalance anytime you feel tense or stressed.

FREEDOM TO MOVE ON

"When we choose to forgive someone, we can also choose not to resume that relationship," Lindsay reminds us. "We can forgive without pretending that everything is the way it was before the hurtful incident. Forgiving someone can take all of our willpower, but the health benefits really are life-giving."

OUR SENSES ARE POWERFUL FORCES OF
ENERGY delivered right into the center of our being.
The things we see, smell, touch, taste, and hear
change our cells, our brain waves, our stomach acids,
and our hearts.

FOCUS ON YOUR SENSES

18

PAMPERING OUR SENSES IS AN EASY WAY TO FEEL INSTANT, DEEP, AND
intense gratification.

Try this as a MomSpa indulgence: Focus on one sense a day.
Truly *see* for a day by looking closely at the wonder of the world
around you. Look closely at the wings of a butterfly, the fur on a
cat, the baby-soft hair on a child.

Move on the next day to truly feel by running your hands
over the different fabrics and surfaces in your house. Then truly
smell, truly *hear*, and don't forget to truly *taste*.

Focusing on such small pleasures will help you focus on the beauty and the joy that is already in your life. Here are some suggestions to get you started:

Heat: Who doesn't love the warmth of a hot bath, the feel of a heat wrap draped around an aching neck, the heat of the sun on her back, or the warmth of a heating blanket on a cold winter's night? Steamy Jacuzzis, hot coffee and tea, fuzzy slippers, warm bear hugs—we could go on and on. Heat in its many forms is instant, affordable, and oh so pleasurable to all aspects of your being.

Fragrance: Some wonderful ways to pamper yourself with scents are with the many scented candles that are available these days, scented lotions, perfumes, and body washes.

Touch: "Fabrics like silk, satin, cashmere, and angora are materials that help us relax and feel sensual." Use a feather bed, satin sheets, or super-fuzzy blankets to turn your bed into heaven on earth.

MomSpa Magic

For a little mood magic, try some aromatherapy. Brighten your mood an dlift your spirits by wearing lavender or rose water perfume, or by sniffing a cottonball dipped in essential oil of rosemary, lavender, clary sage or roses.

ON AN ORDINARY WEDNESDAY JUST AFTER
HER TWO BOYS HAVE BOARDED THE SCHOOL
BUS, Jennifer is already far from home in a Parisian café.
Doesn't that sound wonderful? It does indeed, except that
Jennifer is still sitting in her own living room in California,
several thousand miles from the City of Lights. Her mind has
taken her the distance, transported by the musical sounds
of the French duo Les Nubians playing softly in the background while she sips her latte.

EMBARK ON A MUSICAL VACATION

19

YOU CAN ESCAPE ON A SHORT MENTAL VACATION TO YOUR FAVORITE
exotic destination as easily as slipping in a CD and allowing yourself to dream a bit. Depending on the music and your imaginary
destination, you might even begin to dance and sway around the
room, adding a bit of exercise to the relaxation technique!

What kind of music will transport you? Stay away from the
music you listen to every day, whether that's the pop, country, or

rock music from your youth or the music your kids clamor to listen to. Perhaps it is music that will evoke your honeymoon, or a special trip you have taken in the past? Perhaps music from a country that you dream of visiting some day? Classical music can also inspire a daydream, but if you listen to it on a regular basis, it becomes an ordinary part of your life, one that's not likely to take your mind far away from its present location.

"I've never been to Latin America," Jennifer admits, "although I do hope to go someday. In the meantime, I find Latin music so sexy and relaxing to listen to." Favorites include the Yo-Yo Ma recording *Obrigado Brazil*, filled with haunting cello tango music.

To take a musical vacation, you must *focus* on the music. Don't just use it as a backdrop to your house-cleaning routine! Put on the CD, pour yourself a cup of coffee or tea, and sit down in a comfortable chair to relax and let your mind wander far afield.

Dreaming of a long sea voyage someday? The sound track to the hit movie *Master and Commander* will give you plenty of room to dream. From the eerie sounds of a fog-bound sea to the stirring music that accompanies the battle scenes, you will be transported for the next hour. Equally adventurous daydreaming will result from the sound track to *The Motorcycle Diaries*, as you envision yourself on the back of an ancient motorcycle sputtering along the high roads of the Andes. Can you think of a sound track that will inspire you?

SHOWER THERAPY

YES, a LONG, hoT BaTh iS hEaVEN, a DREamy Way To RELaX aND uNWiND.
But what to do if you have only a few brief moments? Or, like Jennifer, only showers in the house? Deina's aromatherapy shower comes to the rescue for harried women who bathe standing up.

"Before all these fancy devices were invented in the spa industry, there was a fairly simple technique to get scent into a steamy room: Put essential oil on a washcloth and stash it in a corner," Deina tells us. "It's not pretty, but it does the trick."

TO SCENT YOUR SHOWER, ALL YOU NEED TO DO IS TAKE AN EXTRA washcloth, wet it, and drop four or five droplets of your favorite essential oil onto it. Tuck the washcloth into a corner on the floor of the shower. Turn on your shower and let it run on hot for a minute or two to steam things up a bit and disperse the scent into the air (a wasteful use of energy, so don't do this every time you take a shower or your utility bills will suddenly jump!). Then step into your cloud of scented steam. Breathe deeply now, and enjoy the blissful smell.

To extend the healing qualities of your shower, you can bring a small pot of herb-steeped water in with you. Remember MomSpa Indulgence #13, The Herbal Bath (see page 40)? When Deina doesn't have time to let the herbs steep in the tub for 30 minutes, she'll just toss a handful of herbs into a pot of boiling water and let that steep and cool for 15 minutes. Try it, and then bring the herb-infused water along into your scented shower. Dip your washcloth in and scrub down with the herb water so that your skin—as well as your mood—can benefit.

SCENT-SATIONAL SHOWER SCENTS

Citrus scents are wonderful mood lifters—lemon, lime, grapefruit, tangerine, and orange. Other mood-lifting essential oils are bergamot, rosemary, and cardamom. Soothing scents to reduce stress are lavender, clary sage, sandalwood, chamomile, pine, and vetiver.

So much OF WhaT BEEN DESCRIBING So FaR, iNVOLVES SNaTChiNG TimE aWay FRom youR Family iN oRDER TO DO ThiNGS FoR YOURSELF. And as you know, we firmly believe that you should do that. When a mother takes the time to take care of herself, everyone benefits greatly. But you may be wondering, are there small things you can do that will help your mood and give you a special experience that can also involve your kids? You bet. Pack them all in the car and head out to your local farmers' market

THE MORNING MARKET 21

SHOPPING IN LARGE GROCERY STORES CAN BE SO CONVENIENT, WITH everything we need right there all at once. Shopping at a farmers' market, on the other hand, gives us a chance to slow down and stroll through the aisles, reminding ourselves that the food we eat comes from farms and orchards, from people who devote their lives to raising a great and healthful product. The colors, the smells, the sights, the tastes! All combine to create a sensual and earthy way to shop.

To extend your morning meditation into a spa-like afternoon, buy the ingredients for a light lunch from the farmers. Look for a loaf of freshly baked bread, some vine-ripened heirloom tomatoes, and a wedge of handmade cheese. Salad greens, cucumbers, and avocados with small-batch olive oil round out the meal. What could be more delicious?

Don't forget to buy fresh apricots if they're in season. Besides being luscious on their own or sliced on top of ice cream, you can use one to whip up a quick and delicious facial scrub.

WhaT you'LL NEED
Apricot Facial Scrub

- 1   medium apricot
- 1   tablespoon aloe vera juice
- 1   tablespoon honey
- 1   crushed capsule vitamin E
- ½   tablespoon crushed almonds

Puree the skin and flesh of one apricot and the rest of the above ingredients in the blender, or food processor. Rub the scrub gently over your face, leave on for 5 minutes, then rinse off with warm water. You'll smell good enough to eat!

WHAT MOTHER DOESN'T WANT TO LOOK LIKE a MOVIE STAR ON OCCASION, and, even better, be treated like one, too! Tired of looking the same day after day, year after year, Jennifer gathered up all of her makeup and went to the mall one evening. Not to buy all new makeup—that would be far too costly in a house devoted to two small boys. Instead, she was hoping to learn new ways to use what she already had. And to sit and enjoy the all-too-brief feeling of specialness we all get during a makeover.

Yes, having a professional and glamorous makeover at a cosmetics counter is actually free. But it is a woman of strong stuff who can actually sit down, enjoy the free makeover, and then walk off with her wallet intact afterwards. We all feel guilty and end up buying, don't we? Jennifer always springs for at least a lipstick to make the experience seem fair to the makeup artist.

GLAMOUR ON THE CHEAP

SO TRY THIS ONE AFTERNOON OR evening when you feel the need for a beauty perk-up: Go through your cosmetics drawer and determine which department store brand you own the most of. Call ahead to the beauty counter and watch closely as she works her magic, see what she recommends, and treat yourself to a new color or product you're not already using. Next time you put on your makeup you can use your new indulgence and apply what you've learned with the makeup you already have!

TRy ThE comic-Book TRick

It's hard to relax and enjoy being pampered with kids in tow, but it *is* possible. Jennifer brought her two young sons along to the beauty counter, stopping to buy two comic books beforehand. While she perched on the tall stool, her children sat quietly (for once) on the floor beside her, reading away. Give the comic-book method a try if you need to subdue your children in a pinch!

"READ A BOOK." IS THE PAT ADVICE given to so many of us who are seeking a little peace and quiet in our day. Or maybe it is "take a hot bath." And it could be "read a book in a hot bath." Ah, but our MomSpa advice is different: We say, read a book next to a window.

A ROOM WITH A VIEW

23

ONE OF THE PLEASURES OF READING IS THE CHANCE TO CONSIDER WHAT you have read. To mull over what the characters have done (and what you might have done in those circumstances), to think about the twists and turns in the plot (and how they remind you of your own life), to enjoy the satisfaction of coming to the last page, closing the book, and savoring the experience instead of jumping up to rush off and do something else. And that is where a window comes in.

Sit next to a window the next time you sit with a book, and give yourself permission to stop every few pages and gaze out that handy window. If the window has an inspiring view, perfect! It will give you the chance to look at a beautiful and restful scene, to slow your heart rate and decompress. Look closely at the natural aspects of your view, note the variety of shapes and colors in the leaves on any one tree, count the number and types of birds flying by. Remind yourself that while we hustle and run through life, the natural world moves slowly around us as though we didn't exist at all. As though no one were watching.

No window? No inspiring view? Find a poster, a painting, or a print with a fabulous natural scene that you can hang up and focus on when you need to. Jennifer's husband Peter is fond of a watercolor sailing scene of the San Francisco Bay. He can sit and look and think about all manner of things while gazing at that one painting. Find *your* scene!

If you end up doing more gazing then reading, don't worry. It's all good.

Books to Get Lost In

Good books to escape in are books that take us to a different place and time, a place without day care centers and dirty diapers, a time before cell phones and laptops and all manner of high-tech devices. Escape your daily existence with an Edith Wharton novel like *The Age of Innocence*, or travel far back in time with Anita Diamant's *The Red Tent*. Jennifer reads the nineteenth-century novels of Honoré de Balzac—yet another way for her to get to Paris without leaving town!

PICTURE THIS: YOUR FAMILY IS GONE FOR THE NIGHT, and the only person you need to please for the next few hours is . . . you. Sure, sometimes on nights like that we'd like to skip cooking entirely and pop in the Lean Cuisine, but why not treat yourself to a well-planned feast for one?

I used to cook such gourmet meals for myself when I was single and first starting out with my own apartment," Jennifer remembers. "Every afternoon, I'd traipse down to the grocery store and buy something like six fresh scallops, one small onion, and a half bottle of good white wine. Every evening was a mini-feast." As you can imagine, it has been many years since Jennifer bought herself six fresh scallops to cook for dinner!

A FABULOUS FEAST FOR ONE

DON'T PASS UP AN OPPORTUNITY TO CATER to your own tastes instead of worrying about the likes and dislikes of everyone else. For once, you won't have to worry about who likes their steak rare and who likes it well done—just do it

Small Indulgences

Too tired to cook for yourself? Looking for a jazzier treat while the coast is clear? We say take yourself out to your favorite restaurant—you deserve it. Don't worry about feeling self-conscious sitting by yourself—bring a book if you feel the need to keep your head down. Don't let anyone give you a crummy table, though. Speak up if they try to put you in the corner by the kitchen. Enjoy!

exactly the way *you* want it! You don't have to keep track of what vegetable works for everyone. Choose the veggies you like!

If you were at a spa, chances are that the food would be on the light side and the portions would be smallish. Here at MomSpa, we say when these rare opportunities arise, you shouldn't really worry about calories. Go for your own favorite comfort foods, and don't focus on calories—focus on flavor, texture, and temperature. Focus on the all-too-rare feeling of pleasing yourself. Remember how great it feels!

Once you've chosen your just-for-you menu, enjoy the chance to shop for just a few items without worrying about a child melting down in the aisle. Buy fresh. Take your time in the kitchen. Put out your prettiest dishes and search for a linen napkin. Put your favorite music on as loud as you please (remember, this party is just for you), sit down, and tuck in.

SOMETIMES THE BEST MASSAGES ARE GIVEN BY
THE TINY PEOPLE WHO LIVE IN YOUR HOUSE EVERY
DAY—YOUR OWN CHILDREN. Little kids can have
surprisingly wonderful fingers for neck and head massages.
Lindsay accumulates stress in her neck, and her daughters take
turns massaging her neck muscles. "They do a marvelous job!"
Lindsay says. "I know of kids who will massage their mom's feet
and toes, and the moms just love it. Of course, you can't be
too ticklish or this won't work. But the kids try so hard to
please and are so eager, that with a little loving guidance, they
can become your favorite stress-busters!"

Jennifer's children love to be massaged themselves. They will
cozy up on the couch for a little mommy love at night. "I bought
several wooden massage rollers and those plastic Nukkles for
sale at the mall," she says. "We sit in front of the fire during the
winter and everyone gets a turn. It's a great way to spend a family
evening. My two boys are going to make such great husbands!"

MASSAGE WITH KIDS

YOU CAN FILL A BASKET WITH INEXPENSIVE MASSAGE TOOLS AND TENNIS balls (see MomSpa Indulgence #5 on page 24 for ways to use the tennis balls as massage tools). Use them to massage your kids and husband, and teach them how to massage you in return. Don't put massage oils out for the kids to get into, though—you do *not* want your furniture ruined by an enthusiastic mini-masseuse!

SmaLL INDULGENCES

The Nukkles hand massage tool can be used by grown-ups and kids to give an amazing acupressure massage. Check for it at your local health food store, or online at www.comfortchannel.com. Well worth the $20 investment!

ESCAPE THE CRITICS

IT iS So EaSy To LOOK AROUND OUR
LiVES aND FEEL DiSSaTiSFiED WiTh
WhaT WE haVE, unhappy because we don't
have what someone else has, or depressed
because we don't look the way we think we
should. We just don't measure up. Or at least
that is how it's all too easy to feel after a day
spent flipping through glossy magazines, watching television ads and sitcoms, and listening to
the radio. So give yourself a break from the
biggest critic of all—yourself.

AND WHERE DOES THAT VERY HARSH CRITIC—YOU—GET HER IDEAS
about what the standards are? From those same television shows
and ads, from the pages of magazines that display such beauty
and opulence, and in the words and images of the media all
around us.

So, turn it off for a while. To give yourself a break from self-criticism, put a stop to the negative and unhealthy images and ideas you are absorbing from advertising. Yes, you will feel fat and dumpy and unhappy with your body as long as you keep seeing ads that use teeny-tiny teenage models. Quit looking!

Give this a try: See if you can go a whole forty-eight hours without watching TV, reading a magazine, or listening to the radio. Yes, we know that's two whole days. Just try it. Play tag with your kids, read a classic novel, or take a walk instead. You will find that all of the "I want, I need, I don't have" dialogue that plays in your head recedes as the two days pass.

Once you see how good it feels and how much you get done, vow to spend one whole week in which you watch the natural world around you, the birds and the trees and your own children's happy faces, instead of watching television. Not only will you be looking at life a whole different way, but you will soon discover that, without all of the images of perfect people and perfect things to contrast your life to, you are happier with what is around you and who you are.

Skip the self-criticism that is so destructive and seemingly never ends. Accept yourself and your life as they are.

Just Say "No Way!"

Harvard Professor Juliet Schor finds that most television shows are set in the realm of the upper middle class (*Desperate Housewives*, anyone?), so they serve as hour-long exposure to things we want to own but can't really afford. She found that the households with the highest TV viewing rates also had the lowest savings rate. Another reason to turn off the TV!

IF Not lust, then at least luster.

Taking time to treat your hair with an intensive
moisturizing treatment can have a big payoff
when it comes to shine and strength, which might
well inspire lust in others!

LEMON HAIR LUST

27

MAKE A SIMPLE HAIR TREATMENT WITH THE SAME TYPE OF OIL THAT makes such good massage oil—apricot kernel oil.

What you'll Need

Lemon Hair Treatment

2   tablespoons (30 ml) apricot kernel oil
4   drops citrus essential oil

Mix the oils together in a glass bowl. Dip your fingers into the oil and begin to lightly stroke it onto dry (do not wet first) hair. Concentrate on the ends, which are the driest and brittlest parts of your hair. If you have very dry hair, you can apply the oil up to the scalp, but most women benefit from just having the oil on the ends and lower part of the hair strands.

For a more intensive treatment, you can heat the oil by putting it into the microwave for a few seconds (really just a few, like 10 or 15 seconds). Be careful when dipping your fingers into the oil for the first time: Don't heat it so high that you burn your fingers or your scalp! You want it to be pleasantly warm.

Leave the oil on your dry hair for at least 20 minutes before shampooing.

Skip Daily Shampooing

For much of history, people really didn't bathe—first not at all, and then not very often. (Stay with us here—there's a point to this.) Even when they finally began bathing regularly, they seldom washed their hair. So the idea that we need to wash our hair every day is a very, very recent one, and it might not be that healthy for our hair. Go ahead and give your hair a natural beauty treatment by skipping a few days of washing to let your own natural oils do what they are designed to do.

WhEN WaS ThE LaST TimE you PLaNNED or scheduled a small block of time just to reflect on your life? Mothers are so busy, multitasking away and meeting everyone else's needs, that it is easy to miss out on quiet time for ourselves.

TAKING TIME TO TIME-TRAVEL

LINDSAY IS ON THE GO CONSTANTLY, BETWEEN HER SMALL CHILDREN, a thriving home-based business, and a husband who travels Monday through Friday on a regular basis. When the stress level gets too high, though, she intentionally frees up time to rest her mind and let it wander into the past and meander into the future. Here is her method:

"I decided to gift myself with some healthy, unrestricted, unproductive free time to do whatever I want," she tells us. "With my schedule, it has to be early in the morning or late at night. When I can carve out that time, I use it to dream about my passions and how I will pursue them in the future. Travel is one of my dreams, and I long for the day when we can all travel to exotic places as a family. Closing my eyes and letting my mind run free, I envision my family riding camels in Egypt while wearing flowing white robes, exploring the pyramids, and digging for archeological artifacts. Or perhaps I picture us all on an eco-adventure in the deep Brazilian rain forest. Some nights my mind takes us all to the region of Tuscany in Italy to walk the hills and study art and cooking."

Bathtime is perfect for this exotic indulgence. Put your CD player on the toilet lid (or anyplace it will stay safe and dry) and pop in music from the country you plan to visit in your imagination Add bath salts or essential oils that remind you of that country-lavender for France, violet-scented bath beads for England, sandalwood for India. Burn Candles or incense to enhance the mood, sink into the hot, fragrant water, and let your mind wander!

Four-Star Shower

While showering one day with her eyes closed and enjoying the warm water massaging her shoulders, Jennifer had this thought: "I could be anywhere. In any shower, in any house or hotel, in any country. With my eyes closed under a warm shower, I can let my mind wander and picture myself in the shower at a four-star hotel, or in the shower at a custom-built house clinging to an ocean-side cliff, or in the shower in my college dorm." Alone and relaxed in the steamy warm enclosure, you'll agree that it's the perfect time for a mental escape.

.Ah, a WEEKEND AT A SPA ALONE, away from
the cares of the household and the family. How divine.
How elusive. How unrealistic for so many of us. But
wait, there is a way to go to a spa and meet with much
less resistance from your spouse

SPA GETAWAY FOR TWO

JENNIFER HAS STILL NOT WORKED UP THE NERVE TO ANNOUNCE THAT
she is going away to a spa for the weekend. An hour, yes, an
afternoon on occasion, but a whole weekend on her own at a
spa? What she has done, though, is suggest that she and her
husband Peter go together for a weekend to a hotel that has
plenty of things for him to do, and a spa for her!

Don't assume that your husband will scoff at this idea. More and more men are opening up to the idea of spas, massages, and facials. You might be surprised at what he will agree to do! If the idea of getting a massage sounds too wacky for him, ask  if there is a "sports massage" available. Sounds so much more manly, doesn't it?

MomSpa Magic

If a real spa getaway isn't in your immediate future, you can still enjoy the spa experience with your husband. Drop the kids off at grandma's, have the babysitter take them to her place for an afternoon of movies, or arrange a play date at a friend's house. Now, it's your turn to play! Put on mood music, light some candles, and fire up some seductive sandal wood incense (if you both like it). A little sensual slow-dancing is a great way to come down after a long week, then step into the shower. Give each other a full-body scrub. (See MomSpa Indulgence #65 on page 148 for the recipe. Use rosemary rather then rose geranium for a more invigorating scent.) Slowly shampoo each other's hair. Then retreat to the bedroom for a luxurious massage. See MomSpa Indulgence #64 on page 146 for a recipe for homemade massage oil.

Most men wouldn't understand

that there's something about having clean, freshly painted toes that gives women a sexy, I'm-in-the-mood feeling. Sometimes the littlest things we do for ourselves result in the biggest payoff in the pleasure and pamper department (not only for ourselves, but also for our loved ones!).

LIFE'S LITTLE SPLURGES

IMAGINE THAT YOU FINALLY HAVE THE TIME TO SIT IN THE SALON'S pedicure massage chair, turn it on to thump against your lower back, flip idly through a glossy magazine that you never let yourself buy in the grocery store, and sink your feet into that warm, sudsy water. Ahhh…that is heaven indeed. Twenty-five dollars well spent once a month can go a long way to improving your outlook on life!

Spending that $25 and sitting in that massage chair once a *week*, however, not only puts a kink in the family budget, it also dilutes the specialness of the experience. Save these moments of pleasure for rarer occasions, and they will mean more to you when you do indulge.

What? The MomSpa Team urging restraint? Well, here's why: Life's little splurges are worth waiting for, and well worth keeping for those rare occasions when you think the budget can handle it. Just like a too-frequent pedicure spoils the feeling, too-frequent little splurges will dull the pleasure and power to enjoy them when they do happen. (Not to mention those awful feelings of pit-of-the-stomach guilt if you throw off the budget.) When it is time for an indulgence, we say, go for big satisfaction in a small way. Of course, you can treat yourself to a pedicure treatment at home, too. Set out your supplies — cotton socks, a rich peppermint or lavender foot cream (you can make your own by putting a few drops of peppermint or lavender essential oil in any rich cream or lotion), a tub of hot soapy water, fresh towels, and the Lemon Lavender Lift from MomSpa Indulgence #1 on pages xx. Make and use the scrub as described there, wash it off, towel dry, rub your feet and ankles with the rich cream (lavender to soothe, peppermint to stimulate), slathering it on, and then put on the cotton socks to give the cream a chance to really soak in to your scrubbed, softened, heavenly-smelling feet.

PLAY DRESS-UP

31

SHERI BELMONICO, KNOWN TO HER FRIENDS AS GIGI (short for "glamour girl"), loves to spend an evening or afternoon playing dress-up in her own home. Her own MomSpa technique for relaxation is to rummage through her closet and pull out the clothes she already owns to try on in new and different combinations. "In the middle of the day if I'm all alone at home—everyone else in the household is at school or at work— I might stop my chores for a bit and just have an impromptu play session with my clothes. I love clothes, and dressing up makes me happy, but in my small town, I seldom get the chance.

BESIDES HAVING A LITTLE IMAGINATIVE INTERLUDE ON YOUR OWN, YOU can also play dress-up with your friends for a good laugh. "Have your friends bring over the clothes they never get to wear in public! Or go to a friend's house and help her figure out a new outfit for a special occasion," Sheri says.

Sheri points out that to really set the mood when big girls play dress-up, you have to choose the right music to set the tone. "You can't have CNN in the background," she warns.

Jennifer loves this indulgent technique herself, and a few days before a special night out, she can often be found trying on this and that to find just the perfect outfit. "It helps you anticipate a big date night with your husband and lets you get a bit excited in advance," she says. She spent a recent afternoon trying on different black skirts and tops in anticipation of a night at the opera (alone, mind you, without her opera-hating husband). As she rummaged through her closet, she made sure the sounds of the opera swelled around her.

So go ahead and give yourself permission to play around in your own closet. It's cheaper than shopping, and who knows what you might stumble across!

DETOX?! DON'T PANIC, WE DON'T THINK YOU'VE BEEN DRINKING TOO MUCH, but we *do* believe that every so often your body needs a break. A break from all of the heavy foods we all like to indulge in, a break to rest and recuperate and allow our bodies to eliminate a toxin or two. If (and when) you visit a spa, you will find a great deal of emphasis placed on the elimination of toxins, so why not remove a smidge on your own?

DETOX DAYS **32**

JENNIFER IS A COFFEE-GIRL, SELDOM SEEN WITHOUT A MUG FIRMLY IN hand. But she goes cold turkey on a regular basis and lets her body go without the French roast for a solid two weeks. "Replace the coffee with green tea, and your body will appreciate the rest," she says.

To duplicate a spa experience more closely, you can choose a weekend without much competing activity going on and dedicate yourself to detoxing. Twinings of London, the tea company, has developed an easy-to-follow, two-day detox plan. Try our version of their plan, or work out your own using ours as a guideline.

DAY ONE

First thing: Drink a glass of water with a squeeze of fresh lemon juice, and eat a small piece of fresh fruit such as an orange, apple, or apricot.

Breakfast: Choose one of these options:
1. A large bowl of plain or fruit yogurt mixed with a sliced banana, a sprinkling of ground flaxseeds, and a teaspoon of honey or maple syrup.
2. Homemade muesli: The night before, soak two tablespoons of organic oats in four tablespoons of apple juice and two tablespoons of water. Store the mixture overnight in the refrigerator. The next morning, stir in a handful of chopped dried figs, dates, or raisins, walnut pieces, and a grated apple.
Either choice: Drink a cup of green tea with your breakfast.

Mid-morning: Drink a glass of water and eat a small piece of fresh fruit.

Lunch: Make a huge salad with any or all of these ingredients: leaf lettuce (choose darker-green types such as romaine), avocado, broccoli, celery, fresh herbs, carrots, tomatoes, cabbage, and spinach. Whisk up a dressing from one teaspoon extra-virgin olive oil, cider or balsamic vinegar to taste, and salt and pepper to taste.

Mid-afternoon: Have a cup of green tea and some fresh fruit.

Dinner: Make a quick and easy vegetable soup with one organic onion, one clove of garlic, one teaspoon extra-virgin olive oil, two large carrots, one small head of broccoli, and salt and pepper to taste. In a soup pot, sauté the onion and garlic in the olive oil. Wash and chop the carrots and broccoli, add them to the soup pot, season with salt and pepper, and cover with water. Simmer until the vegetables are tender, about twenty minutes. Allow the soup to cool before pouring it into a blender or food processor. Puree the soup, then reheat and serve.

Before bed: Relax, digest, and unwind with a cup of decaffeinated green tea or a restful herb tea such as chamomile tea.

DAY TWO
First thing: Have a teaspoon of flaxseed oil and chase it with a large glass of water.

Breakfast: Choose either a large fruit salad or a shake made by blending one large banana, a teaspoon of cream, a dozen blanched almonds, a teaspoon of dark honey, and ½ cup of water until smooth and frothy.

Mid-morning: Eat a few dried plums, figs, or apricots and a handful of unsalted nuts, such as pistachios, almonds, or hazelnuts (not peanuts). Enjoy a cup of green tea.

Lunch: Choose either leftover soup from yesterday, or a salad made from any of the ingredients in yesterday's lunch list. As a sweet and nourishing extra, sprinkle the salad with a few raisins.

Mid-afternoon: Have a large cup of green tea.

Dinner: Choose either grilled fresh fish with a large green salad, or a generous serving of chèvre (goat cheese) crumbled over a large green salad. Enjoy a cup of jasmine green tea.

Before bed: Have a small cup of plain or fruit yogurt.

After two days of this light and nutritious eating plan, you should feel relaxed and energized. The point is not weight loss as much as it is giving your digestive system a small but much-needed break

Take It Easy!

We don't recommend doing much in the way of exercise on these days. Simple yoga stretching is fine, but stay out of the hot box yoga routine, because if you're used to heavier foods, your body might feel weak.

CHEAPER THAN A SHRINK, MORE
PRIVATE THAN A CRY WITH A GIRLFRIEND,
and all over in a mere two-and-a-half hours.
Sometimes a good tearjerker of a movie is just what
the MomSpa doctor ordered.

A GOOD LONG CRY

33

YOU CAN INDULGE IN A WEEP-FEST AT NIGHT AFTER YOUR FAMILY IS IN
bed, or on those rare nights when you suddenly have the house
to yourself. Either way, for maximum weepiness and maximum
relaxation, stay away from the creepy stalking movies, true
crime, science fiction, and horror. Also stay away from any
movie where children are in peril, and, depending on what is
going on in your real life, stay away from anything that might
replicate your own circumstances. The point is to lose yourself
for a few short hours in someone else's romance, in someone
else's life.

Crying is good for the soul and, no matter how happy your life is, a good cry always makes you feel better. As women, we know that. When the chance arises, you might want to invite a friend or two to weep along with you. Or you might prefer to have a therapeutic cry all on your own. Pull the curtains, pop up some popcorn (indulging in real butter, of course!), snuggle up on your couch, and sniffle away.

To get you started, here are a few of the MomSpa Team's recommendations for great weepy romantic movies. Add your own favorites to the list!

Beaches
The Bridges of Madison County
The End of the Affair
The English Patient
Ghost
Love Story
Somewhere in Time
Titanic
The Way We Were
You've Got Mail

FRANKLY, MY DEAR.

We all have something to learn from one of the all-time greatest weepy movies: *Gone with the Wind*. Scarlett might be a teensy bit self-centered, but we can all follow her example and learn how to use our ingenuity when the budget is tight but a big event is looming. Scarlett, of course, turned her curtains into a ball gown. (This might not be quite as glamorous if we're using our insulated thermal curtains, but just think of the effect if you use sheers!)

CAN YOU BELIEVE WE NOW LIVE IN A
WORLD WHERE WE CAN BUY AROMATHERAPY
PRODUCTS TO CLEAN OUR BATHROOMS?

Unbelievable, but true. In addition to using scented
candles to set the mood, scented face mist to seal in
moisture, and scented lotions to unwind, we can all use
scented herbal cleaning products to give even scrubbing
the bathroom an aura of spa glamour!

AROMATHERAPY CLEANING SUPPLIES

HIGH-END STORES NOW SELL LAUNDRY SOAPS WITH INCREDIBLE SCENTS
like lemongrass, Meyer lemon, and cucumber mint. At around $20,
these kinds of products are really too pricey for everyday use, but
they're fun to use for a special treat. Perhaps, after returning from a
family vacation, you can wash your clothes in scented soap to continue the feeling of being somewhere special. These soaps leave
only a very mild scent on your clean clothes, but they do make
your laundry room smell delightful while the load is running.
And here are three make-it-yourself concoctions to brighten your
cleaning routines:

What You'll Need

Lavender Vacuuming Powder

  1 cup (220 g) baking soda
  ¼ cup dried lavender flower buds

Jennifer bought a $9 bottle of lavender vacuum powder at the famous Pike Street Market in Seattle, and promptly figured out how to duplicate it for far less money: Just add dried lavender buds to baking soda, crumbling them between your fingers to separate the seeds from the stem. Store your homemade powder in an old salt shaker or a plastic shaker, and sprinkle the powder on your carpet 10 minutes or so before vacuuming. You'll notice a wonderful scent while you're running your vacuum cleaner back and forth across the crushed lavender.

Lavender Dryer Bags

  1 cup dried lavender flower buds
  1 cotton muslin drawstring bag (you can find them at craft stores)

You can also use lavender in your dryer. Pour 1 cup of dried lavender buds into a small muslin bag, draw the strings tight, and toss it into the dryer along with your wet clothes. Each bag is good for 3 or 4 drying sessions, then just dump out the old lavender (you can compost it if you want) and pour in a cup of fresh dried lavender buds. Again, it is a fairly subtle scent, but a lovely little touch.

Aromatherapy Dish Soap

     1 bottle inexpensive dish soap
8 to 12 drops essential oil

To make doing dishes a tiny bit more pleasant, Deina makes her own scented dish soap. "I buy very inexpensive dish soap and add 8 to 12 drops of essential oils like lavender, lime, or orange," she says. "I love the smell, and I know that the oils kill germs, too."

BRIGHT EYES

35

DARK CIRCLES ARE A PROBLEM FOR ALL OF US, ESPECIALLY THOSE MOMS WHO ARE STILL UP AT NIGHT WITH SMALL CHILDREN! Dark circles can appear for several reasons in addition to lack of sleep: They could be caused by a lack of vitamins, or they might even be hereditary. Deina has several methods she developed in her years of running day spas that can help minimize the raccoon look.

"SHOCK THOSE CIRCLES WITH ICE! IT REALLY AWAKENS THE SKIN AND increases blood circulation," she suggests. Okay, don't actually put a piece of ice on your eye. Instead, do it this way:

Apply toner or astringent to small pieces of gauze, put them in a resealable bag, and store them in the freezer. The gauze gets cold and crisp and ready for action. When you wake up in the morning or just before you are ready to go out somewhere special, hit the freezer, take one piece of gauze for each eye, and apply over your (closed) eyes. Wow! That cool application increases blood circulation and helps reduce dark puffiness around the eyes.

MomSpa Magic

Jennifer's martini variation on the icy gauze idea (she did write *The Martini Diet*, after all) is to use inexpensive vodka as your skin toner, add a drop of lemon essential oil, and soak the gauze pads in that. Then pop them into the freezer as described above. The effect of the frozen pads is the same, but it smells like a cocktail party and gets you into the evening mood!

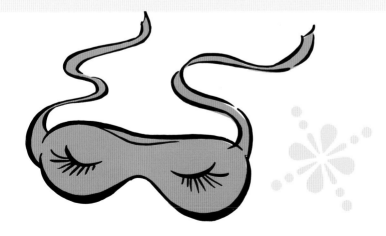

YOU'VE SEEN THE ADVICE IN WOMEN'S
MAGAZINES COUNTLESS TIMES: Leave
thoughtful little love notes in your children's lunch
sacks and your husband's briefcase. A sweet and
thoughtful gesture, to be sure, but wait a minute . . .
who is leaving attagirl notes for *you*? Looks like you
might have to take matters into your own pen.

LOVE NOTES TO YOU!

36

MOMS ARE DRAINED OF ENERGY ON A DAILY BASIS, AND BY THE END OF the day, our emotional bank account can end up empty. Keeping a positive mental attitude and acknowledging that our capabilities are vast and our possibilities are endless will help keep things in perspective. We all try to be positive with our children when we discipline or instruct, but do we apply those same rules to the words we use with ourselves? Probably not. We need to apply those same positive rules to ourselves and remember to watch the words we use when we talk to ourselves.

And for the nicest boost of all, we do need to leave ourselves little positive notes of encouragement. Go ahead and write yourself a love note; say something really positive like "Today I deserve to relax!" or "Hey gorgeous, looking good!" Sure, you will feel silly. But it will be fun thinking of positive things and compliments you can give yourself, and just as much fun to stumble upon them tucked in your underwear drawer. When you feel good about yourself, others will feel good around you. It is a gift for you and for your family!

HAPPY FEET

37

By THE END OF THE DAY, YOU ARE
DRAGGING. You've cleaned your house,
dressed your children, shown up at the office,
cooked a big meal, and now your day is *done*.
Why not relax and cap it off by giving yourself a "feet treat"?

What You'll Need
"Feet Treat" Foot Soak
A large soup pot (large enough for both feet)

¼ cup (70 g) Epsom salts

5 drops essential oil (or a spritz of your favorite perfume)

A big fluffy towel

Fill the pot with the hottest water you can stand, and add the Epsom salts and drops of essential oil. Stir to dissolve the salts and distribute the oil. If you want to use your favorite perfume scent instead of an essential oil, go ahead. Tap a few drops of perfume into the water, or spray the surface once or twice with an atomizer. Soak your bare feet for at least 8 minutes, longer if you have the time, before drying off and wrapping them up in your fluffy towel. We'd recommend leaving the TV off while you do this, and instead putting your head back and letting your mind drift off into a pleasant image of your own making. A favorite vacation? A romantic rendezvous? Use any image you'd like to help you turn off your "mommy mind" and focus more on your own relaxation.

Fragrant Feet
Deina's favorite foot soak includes drops of peppermint oil and basil oil. "In the summer months, it's my favorite way to stay cool and reinvigorate myself," she says. "Those smells just make me come alive!" Try it and see if you agree!

HERE'S AN IDEA: A SPECIAL BREAKFAST OUT WITH THE KIDS ON THE WEEKEND.

Sure, you probably do it every month or so anyway. But here's the MomSpa version: Dad takes the kids out to breakfast and you stay home! You'll need to speak up and let him know what you have in mind. Then you might need to gas up the car, look up the address of the restaurant, and load up the car with children. But you stay put right there in the driveway, waving and smiling as they motor on down the road.

WEEKEND WISDOM 38

JUST THINK WHAT YOU COULD DO WITH two hours to yourself on a Saturday morning! Wait, don't pick up that vacuum! Please don't clean in the precious time you have available; spend it on your own valuable needs.

All those easy beauty treatments you've been reading about here in MomSpa? Get busy and try them! Pull out your Instant Getaway suitcase (MomSpa Indulgence #5, page 24) stuffed with your favorite high-end lotions and your fluffy white spa robe, pop in the CDs you've chosen for your Musical Vacation (MomSpa Indulgence #19, page 52), or head out to a local farmers' market (MomSpa Indulgence #21, page 56) to breathe in the incredible scents of fresh produce.

Whatever you do in those scant hours, enjoy it. Spend them doing what you love the most (and we know that isn't cleaning out your refrigerator). We admit it: We can't really relax either unless the house is clean and tidy. So instead of wasting precious indulgence time dusting your cupboards, do whatever you need to do the night before. Then you'll be pleased with the way your house looks the next morning, and you will be ready to relax the minute you hear the car door slam.

Small Indulgences

If you feel like doing a tiny bit of cooking in your free time, why not make an indulgent treat like chocolate-dipped strawberries? Your family will be thrilled to find them on their return (and they will never guess how many of the sweet things you popped in your mouth while they were gone!). Simply wash and dry a box of fresh strawberries, leaving the hulls on to grasp as you dip. In the top of a double boiler, place 1 cup (175g) of semisweet chocolate chips and 1 teaspoon of Crisco, and melt. Once the chocolate cools down but is still soft enough to coat the berries, pinch those strawberries between your fingers and dip away.

SOME OF THE MOST RESTFUL ASPECTS OF A SPA VISIT ARE THE TINY TOUCHES OF BEAUTY scattered throughout the facility, from the alcoves lit by candles and the carefully arranged, freshly picked blooms in a lovely vase, to the icy cold pitchers of water filled with slices of oranges and lemons. Many of these touches can be duplicated in your own home to create a spa-like feel, and adding more water is the easiest of all!

TAKE THE WATERS
39

YOU MIGHT ALREADY HAVE A BEAUTIFUL CUT CRYSTAL WATER PITCHER, perhaps packed away with those wedding gifts you never got around to using? If so, drag it out into the daylight and dust it off. If you don't already have a lovely water pitcher, go out right this minute and get one. Scout out garage sales and flea markets, keeping an eye peeled for someone else's grandmother's cut crystal water pitcher. It would be a fun treasure-hunt item for a Saturday morning with the kids, driving from one sale to another on the lookout for a gleaming treasure.

Scouting out the housewares sections of discount retailers can also yield cut crystal pitchers at vastly reduced prices. Even allowing yourself a personal indulgence and buying a gleaming crystal water pitcher from Tiffany and Company really isn't *that* extravagant (compared to the price of their diamonds, anyway); check their Web site if you need convincing.

Once you have selected your water pitcher, fill it halfway with filtered water. Slice an orange and a lemon into very thin slices and add them to the water. Fill the remainder with ice cubes. Soon the water will take on the delicious taste of citrus, and the pitcher will turn ice cold and glossy with moisture. Your mouth will water every time you look at it.

Now, choose a prominent spot in your house for your lovely water pitcher. Make sure you place a coaster or a solid trivet under it, as the moisture could wreck your wooden tables. You want to choose a spot that you pass often throughout the course of your day, a place where you will be reminded to stop and pour yourself a glass of that heavenly spa water to perk yourself up. Be sure to put your best glass out with your pitcher to complete the look. (Warning: The idea is to put your beautiful pitcher and glass where *you* will see them often, not where your kids can knock them over!)

How much water should you drink? Despite the vast quantities we've all been consuming these past few years (eight ounces eight times a day), recently scientists have suggested that you really don't need quite that much. But the sight and smell of your citrus water will encourage you to drink water all day long. Bottoms up!

JUST LIKE ENCOURAGING YOUR HUSBAND OR PARTNER TO TAKE THE KIDS OUT FOR BREAKFAST (FAR, FAR AWAY) (our MomSpa Indulgence #38 on page 92) here is another simple idea for freeing up more time to relax, but this time, it's in the evenings. We like to cook healthy, interesting, and creative dinners for our families, and we know you do, too. On occasion, though, a shortcut or two can get you out of the kitchen much faster, with far less stress and the rare chance to spend some time on yourself.

MAKE A SIMPLE PLAN

ANNOUNCE EARLY IN THE DAY THAT YOU HAVE PLANS FOR YOURSELF, and that dinner will be simple. Very simple. So simple that all you plan to do is pick up one of those already roasted chickens from the grocery store, pop some frozen veggies into the microwave, pour a few glasses of milk, and boom—that's it!

When we try to be the perfect moms, sometimes we achieve it. But all too often, we fall short by our own estimation and end up feeling worse than we did before we set the bar so darn high! So one or two days a month, go right ahead and set the bar very, very low for yourself. Give yourself permission to use every cheat and convenience known to woman to get through the daily tasks at hand in order to carve out an extra hour for yourself in the day.

Harried moms can also resort to a "breakfast night" in a pinch. No, this doesn't mean convincing your husband to take the kids out for breakfast at night, but instead allowing them to each pour a bowl of cereal and fruit as an acceptable dinner once in a blue moon. Imagine cutting out all of the stress of dinner prep and most of the stress of cleanup! Better than meditation or a yoga class, trust us.

What to do with your newfound free time? Pick your favorite MomSpa Indulgence — give yourself a facial, a foot or hand treatment, a hair treatment. Or use the extra time to have the kids give you a massage. (See MomSpa Indulgence #25 on page 64).

What, No Pizza?

Sure, you could just order pizza in for everyone on a lazy night like this. But filling up on pizza just before spending time pampering yourself is an odd combination. Sticking to a lighter, less greasy meal is not only healthier, but it helps you pretend that you are in a swanky spa somewhere, waiting to be called for your hot rock massage.

AS WE MENTIONED IN THE INTRODUCTION, WE THREE MomSpa GALS EACH hAVE OUR OWN FAVORITE WAY TO FEEL PAMPERED. Deina indulges in a beauty treatment or two, Lindsay stretches and bends with her yoga poses, and Jennifer...well, Jennifer likes her pearls and her cashmere. Or diamonds and silk. Truthfully, her jewelry box doesn't weigh much (not as much as it does in her imagination, anyway), but she does love the way luxurious fabrics feel on her skin.

PJS AND PEARLS 41

JENNIFER'S FAVORITE WAY TO RELAX AND FEEL PAMPERED IN HER OFF-hours as a wife and mother is to put on her silkiest jammies and drape herself with her shiniest costume jewelry before draping herself across the couch with a favorite book or a glossy magazine. She does wait until everyone else in the house has gone to bed before emerging in all her pseudo-celeb glamour (lest they all giggle loudly at the sight).

Why not indulge in an hour of pretending that you have a whole different lifestyle, one in which photographers lie in wait hoping to snap your gorgeous self, staff hovers around anxiously catering to your every whim, and no one will be calling your name in the middle of the night, asking for a drink of water. Ah, we can only dream…

To further indulge in a little princess fantasy for grown-up girls, you could rent *The Princess Diaries* on DVD and invite your young daughters to join you on the couch in their pajamas and plastic pearls. Pink nail polish for everyone!

MoRE FaNTaSy FLiCkS

Other great movies to indulge a little fantasy life are *The Princess Bride* and *Pirates of the Caribbean*. But fun as it is to watch these costume dramas, we can all be thankful we don't have to drag ourselves around in our everyday mommy lives wearing such heavy dresses!

WE GAVE YOU A FEW QUICK BEAUTY TIPS
FOR USING OLIVE OIL IN THE KITCHEN in MomSpa
Indulgence #8, Kitchen Quickies (page 30). Olive oil can be one of
your best friends in the kitchen when it comes to both healthful
cooking *and* natural beauty. To that we'd like to add another good
kitchen friend—honey.

42

OLIVE OIL AND HONEY BEAUTY

BUT LET'S GET BACK TO OLIVE OIL FOR A MINUTE. "OLIVE OIL HAS
wonderful qualities, but one tiny drawback," Deina warns. "It
smells." What smells wonderful in a salad or a marinade can be
kind of weird on your person. Adding a drop or two of essential
oil to olive oil before you use it in any nonfood beauty kind of
way is the answer, so keep that in mind.

Try rubbing small quantities of olive oil into your cuticles and onto your nails to soften skin and strengthen nails. You can also pour a small quantity of olive oil (use the cheap stuff for this, please) into a dish, add a drop of lemon oil or other scented oil, and then dip your fingers in and give them a good soaking for 20 to 30 minutes. You don't really need to rinse afterwards—just wipe thoroughly with a dish towel so that a thin layer remains behind on your skin.

Honey is a natural tenderizer and helps to hydrate the skin. The simplest use for a squeeze bottle of honey is to leave it next to your bathtub and give it a good squirt whenever you are running hot water. About ½ cup (85 g) of honey is the right amount for a full bathtub. Here are 2 other indulgent home spa treatments that smell great (can't beat that delicious honey fragrance) and work well:

What You'll Need
Milk and Honey Mask
A simple face mask made from honey calls for only two things:

- 2 tablespoons (40 g) honey
- 2 teaspoons (10 ml) milk

Mix the honey and milk together and spread the mixture on your face. You can also use it on the backs of your hands to hydrate and moisturize. Leave it on for 20 minutes before rinsing with warm water.

Olive Oil and Honey Hair Treatment

You can use olive oil and honey together in a hair mask for shiny and lustrous hair.

½ cup (170 g) honey
2 tablespoons (28 g) olive oil

Mix the honey and olive oil together and apply to your dry hair, starting first with your dried-out and split ends and working up. Once you have worked the treatment into your hair, wrap and secure a towel around your hair to keep the oil off your clothes and furniture. Leave the treatment on for at least 20 minutes before shampooing as usual.

MomSpa Tip: Whenever you are shampooing an oil treatment out of your hair, put the shampoo onto your hair first, before adding water. Jennifer learned this beauty trick years ago from Philip Berkovitz, the owner of luxury shampoo manufacturing company Philip B.

PEachy KEEN

Summertime peaches are irresistible under any circumstances, and they, too, have wonderful beauty-product potential. Jennifer is quite fond of pie (*quite* fond), and while making it, she rubs one fresh slice of peach over her face and lets the fruit acids do their thing for a full twenty minutes before rinsing, leaving her with smoother, softer, younger-looking skin. You can also gather up the peelings and rub them on your face for a homemade fruit scrub.!

HERE'S SoMEThiNG you aLREaDy
KNOW: Few things thrill a woman as deeply as
having someone else clean her house. Sweet,
sweet bliss.

SEND IN THE MAIDS!

BUT FOR THOSE OF US ON A SMALLISH HOUSEHOLD BUDGET, THAT BLISS
seldom comes. Until now, when the MomSpa Team fills you in
on this awesome plan:

1. Clean out. First, clear your house of excess clutter and stuff—
old things that no one has used in years, new things you never got
around to taking out of the box, things you don't remember why
you own in the first place. Be brutal: Set a goal of reducing your
clutter by at least 20 percent. It helps to have someone else work
with you on this task, a friend or relative who has no idea why you
still have a bridesmaid dress from 1994 hanging in your closet and
is willing to toss it on a "to go" pile. What you are trying to
achieve is a more restful environment with less stuff to trip over.
Your other goal is to raise some quick cash…

2. Turn a profit. So, to raise some quick extra cash, you can now haul all of your extra unwanted things out into your driveway, put price tags on everything, sit in a lawn chair with a mug of tea, and watch other people clutter up their lives with the things you are now ridding yourself of.

3. Hire the cleaners! Okay, now that you have an extra $150 in hand, you can call in a one-time cleaning service to get your house spic and span and send you into bliss.

Imagine how wonderful it will feel to accomplish two things at once—rid your life of clutter and unnecessary possessions, *and* have a cleaning service come in and put your house in order. Makes you smile just thinking about it, doesn't it?

Once you get the hang of this technique, you might find yourself turning to it on a yearly basis. Plan along with your girlfriends to put on a large-scale community garage sale to increase the turnout and your potential bottom line.

ASK FOR IT!

It's hard to admit that you need help around the house. Some women are even embarrassed to bring the topic up to their husbands. Don't be. If a cleaning service is all it will take to gain a little personal peace and stress reduction, go for it. Kathy Fitzgerald Sherman feels so strongly about this topic that she wrote a book, *A Housekeeper Is Cheaper Than a Divorce: Why You Can Afford to Hire Help and How to Get It*. You might find some good ideas there on how to bring up the subject successfully.

Do you have a favorite spot in your house, a room or a corner that is just the way you like it, filled with the things that make you happy? If so, good for you! If not, well, you might have to go outside to find the peace you need.

OUTDOOR RETREATS

44

CREATING A SMALL SPOT IN YOUR BACKYARD FOR QUIET REFLECTION IS a great goal, and it's getting easier all the time. Whereas in past years you might have had to hire a builder to create a retreat spot, now garden shops are full of tented pavilions, outdoor umbrellas, and plug-in water features like small waterfalls and bubbling stone jars.

Jennifer built a small stone patio herself in a corner of her front yard overlooking an herb garden. Clearing the dirt and setting the stones down in sand was all it took. She added two comfortable chairs and a table large enough for a coffee mug, and placed garden candle holders around the edge. At night, when the candles are lit, it is a fantasy retreat in a spot where the scent of lavender and rosemary fills the air. During the day, it is a peaceful spot to sit with the newspaper before the family wakes up and her mommy duties begin.

All you really need to create an outdoor retreat is a shady spot and a cushioned chair. A patio is nice, a deck is nice, but if all you can do is clear out a patch of dirt in your garden and put in bricks or slate so that your chair doesn't sink into the dirt when you sit down, you're good to go. Depending on the weather in your area, you could bring all kinds of other things out on a semipermanent basis, from a radio tuned to your favorite station to a small bookshelf filled with your favorite books, magazines, and journals. You can bring a lamp outside (use a yellow bug bulb) and add a small rug. (Take them back inside when you go in so it doesn't rain on them.) If you don't have a garden to sit near, some potted plants around your comfy chair can add a more restful feeling.

You can create your outdoor retreat around a theme. A Zen-like retreat might have dark slate tiles, a pile of cushions, and bright green and blue ceramic jars. A French country retreat might have painted yellow chairs, a pot of lavender, and a wide market umbrella. Release your inner decorator and have fun!

One of the blessings of having an outdoor retreat is that you can be outside alone with your thoughts, while your children are safely inside napping or playing. It lets you be "away" without really being away.

SmaLL INDULGENCES

Outdoor kitchens with large barbecues and fire pits are the latest design craze. You don't have to spend a zillion dollars to get the same cozy feeling of hanging out in your backyard at night, though. Just buy one of those inexpensive copper fire pots for outdoor use and enjoy.

WE'VE TALKED A LOT ABOUT BATHS HERE, ABOUT THE GLORY AND WONDER OF A LONG, HOT, SOLITARY SOAK. The chance to soak the tension out of your body, the chance to have some rare quiet time to yourself, to listen to the soothing music of your choice, to smell the delicious scents rising up from the water. Mmmm...

BASIC BATH SOAK 45

ONCE YOU GET THE HANG OF MIXING UP YOUR OWN BATH SALTS, YOU will never again buy a commercial product. Here is the simple secret that will let you mix and match scents to your individual taste. Just memorize this easy formula: 50 percent Epsom salts, 50 percent sea salt, and a few drops of the scent of your choice. Store your personal formula in a glass jar and it is ready to use.

Soak in Salt?

Epsom salt isn't really salt—at least, not the kind you sprinkle on your dinner. Instead, it is a magnesium sulfate mined in Epsom, England, since the seventeenth century. Salt normally dries your skin, but dissolved in gallons of bath water, Epsom salt doesn't have that effect. Rather, it makes your water feel silkier and smoother, less harsh. Epsom salt also helps the body detoxify, soothe, swollen feet, and relieves aching muscles and joints.

Depending on your mood, you might want to use lavender and rosemary oils to relax, or Deina's favorite combo of peppermint and basil to perk up. Enjoy mixing and matching the essential oils to your mood, and you will soon have your own apothecary of bath soaks lined up and ready to use at the edge of your tub.

Salting It Away

Looking for a home-based business idea? If you live in a popular tourist area, you can easily create a bath product that evokes the region and could sell to tourists. For Carmel, California, or anywhere along a woodsy coast, you could add a few drops of eucalyptus oil and then decorate the jar with a tiny pinecone or two. Voilà—Carmel Bath Salts. For the Pacific Northwest, you could use the essence of Noble fir, sweetened with just a hint of citrus. For Florida, make the citrus the key note—as in Key lime. Think about the fragrances that make your area unique—magnolias, anyone?—and take it from there. Just be sure your bath salts smell as good as they look before you bring them to market! Don't forget that these salts make great gifts for friends and relatives, too.

YOU DIDN'T REALLY NEED US TO TELL
YOU in MomSpa Indulgence #43 how great it is
to have someone else clean your house, and
you don't need us to tell you how incredible a
professional massage is. But, like house cleaning,
massage can be costly!

MORE MASSAGE, LESS MONEY

46

MAYBE YOU WILL WANT TO DEDICATE THE PROCEEDS OF YOUR GARAGE
sale to a professional massage instead of a once-a-year house
cleaning. At $100, the price range is about the same for both.
Finding cheaper cleaners is tough, but finding a bargain massage
is easy.

In order to become licensed massage therapists, students not
only have to attend massage school for a lengthy period, they
must also perform hundreds of hours of massage. At the school
in Jennifer's northern California community, a massage performed by an advanced student (who has given more than twenty massages) is $38 an hour. To get a massage from a student

who has performed more than seventy-five massages and is on his or her way to graduation, costs $48 an hour. Compared to a spa price of well over $100 an hour, student massages are an incredible bargain.

Look in the Yellow Pages under "massage therapy schools" in your local phone book to find one near you. At these prices, moms deserve to book monthly massages! You can celebrate all of your major milestones with a massage, not just birthdays. Perhaps the end of soccer season, too!

Not only are massages less expensive through a massage school, but many other beauty treatments are as well, if you seek them out on a student level. Facials and hair care can be found for less at beauty colleges. Manicures and pedicures are also available for bargain rates compared to rates at a regular shop.

As you know, our philosophy is that you deserve to spend the money to indulge yourself for these things, but if you can spend *less money*, then you can indulge *more often*!

The Fine Old Art of Barter

Jennifer helped a masseuse write a marketing brochure in exchange for several hour-long massages, and her husband has traded small building projects for sports massages. What skill do you have? Babysitting? Cooking a dinner or two? Helping with tax forms? You may well have a skill that can gain you a bit of extra pampering. To find a masseuse in your area who might be open to trades, check out the bartering section of www.craigslist.org.

MoST BUSy momS haVE a haRD TimE JUST BEiNG STiLL. To be quiet both in body and in mind is an art some people refer to as meditation. Research shows that slowing ourselves down has many restorative and health benefits. It could even slow down the aging process (we can only hope!).

TAKE YOUR BODY OUT OF MOTION

47

LINDSAY MAKES IT A POINT TO TAKE HER BODY OUT OF MOTION ON A regular basis. Here are some of her tricks to make this easier than you ever thought possible. Try all three and see which ones work best for you!

1. Find a pool and bring a raft. One of the most relaxing activities imaginable is floating motionless on an inflatable rubber or plastic raft in a lake or pool. As the raft molds to the contours of your body, close your eyes and let the gentle swaying movements rock you into a state of bliss.

2. Just sit. Sometimes this is the hardest thing of all for moms to do. We sit down for a second and suddenly spy a dirty sock under the couch, or remember a phone call we need to make, or hear the buzzer go off on the dryer. And up we go, off to take care of something important. Instead, give yourself permission to sit quietly for a few minutes and empty your mind. Leave a book near a chair that will help you escape for a few minutes at a time. "I once read a book that described the north coast with such vivid detail I could feel the mist coming in off the ocean," Lindsay remembers with pleasure. "What a mental vacation that was!"

3. Meditate. Lastly, meditation is an excellent way to relax your body. It's not an easy activity to start, but using a relaxation tape can help. "I've learned to relax naturally with meditations that use guided imagery relaxation techniques to tap into the healing powers of my mind," Lindsay says. "If I'm left on my own to hum or chant a mantra, I end up thinking of too many things and can't concentrate on clearing my mind. You don't have to be a Buddhist to meditate, by the way. It doesn't have to be religion-based at all." One of Lindsay's friends had her own meditation method: She'd go into her walk-in closet and put on a meditation tape. The kids were told not to disturb her until she came out of the closet. We should all have such big closets!

Imagine a morning like this: You awaken gently to the sound of classical music, you slip out of bed and into your favorite loose clothes, splash a little water on your face, and head out the door. Not to go far, just out to your garden to start the day amidst beauty and natural calm. To stand with a steaming cup of coffee in hand, watching the sun rise over your garden, watching the greenery come to life as the warm light hits it, smelling the fresh soil and the healthy herbs, watching insects stir and begin to move. The sights, the sounds, and the smells of a garden early in the morning are a waking meditation. Birds, lizards, bugs . . . maybe a sleepy cat. Scented roses and herbs. The orange, purple, pink, and gold tones in the sky as the sun slowly emerges.

EARLY MORNING IN THE GARDEN

48

ON A DAY WHEN YOU KNOW YOU ARE HEADED FOR A STRESSFUL TIME, why not set your alarm early, set the automatic coffee maker, put your slippers next to your bed, and vow to watch the sun rise from your garden perch? It gives you a quiet time to reflect on the challenges you have to face, whether they involve family or business, and lets you gather your thoughts and gird for the stress to come. Later on, in the midst of your day, you will be able to close your eyes and picture in your mind's eye the beauty of the moments that you witnessed just a few short hours ago.

Just watching the sun rise is a way to start your day off on a calm and peaceful note. Spending a few minutes actually working in your garden is equally enjoyable private time. Jennifer likes to stop in her front yard and pull a few small weeds on her way to pick up the newspaper. Not only is it cool and brisk so early in the morning (unlike the sweaty weed-pulling that happens later in the day), it lets her focus on a small natural process—the cycle of life—that is largely hidden during the rest of our activities throughout the day.

If you have an herb or vegetable garden, you can turn your morning stroll into a culinary adventure. Pick some fresh herbs for your mid-morning tea—one or more types of mint (such as orange mint and peppermint), lemon balm, chamomile, or lemon thyme. Harvest cherry tomatoes, basil, chives, and the most tender lettuce leaves you can find for a fresh salad at noon. Check to see if the corn or summer squash is ready for tonight's dinner. We guarantee you'll feel a renewed sense of well-being with your own homegrown produce in hand!

DEINA LOOKS FORWARD TO "NIGHT NIGHT" TIME WITH HER CHILDREN and likes to do what she can to make sure they drop off to sleep easily. "I don't know how to sew, but I got the idea to make up some tiny pillows with lavender in them to slip inside my children's pillows and encourage sleep," she says.

LAVENDER RICE PILLOWS 49

DEINA SCOUTED OUT HER LOCAL CRAFT STORES AND DOLLAR STORES until she found small baby pillowcases. She then bought several bags of rice (one bag per pillow) and gathered up lavender from her yard to dry. "I filled up each baby pillow with rice and one-half cup of dried lavender flowers," she says. "Then, with my simple stitching skills, I folded the end of each pillowcase over twice and stitched up the end of the pillowcase by hand. They were ready to use! Each pillow cost me around $4 to make, and I love giving them away as gifts!" In addition to using them as a natural sleep aid for her children, Deina slips the pillows into her own pillow and her husband's.

A strong word of warning: Deina's children are no longer tiny babies, so there is no fear of choking, but you would not want to put a pillow with hard small kernels of rice in a small child's bed. Wait until your children are at least 4 years old.

Now that you have a floppy bag filled with rice and lavender, what else can you do with it? Here are two other MomSpa indulgent ideas from Deina:

1. Sore Muscle Soother. Heat the pillow for a minute in the microwave, turn and heat again for another minute. Place the warm scented pillow on top of your aching muscles and relax. You might need two or three pillows, depending on where you hurt!

2. Soothing Eye Pillows. Deina also made some lavender pillows that were smaller by cutting a baby pillowcase in half. She wanted to have small bags that were just the right size for eye treatments. "I made myself two small eye pillows," she says. "I keep one in my nightstand drawer, and before I go to sleep, I place it on my eyes for 15 minutes. This helps me relax and feel pampered. I also keep one small pillow in the freezer. The days I experience puffiness around my eyes, I use the cooling herb bag to reduce the swelling. I lie down and leave it over my eyes for 15 minutes, and my eyes feel refreshed and clear again." (See MomSpa Indulgence #35 on page 86 for more great homemade treatments for puffy eyes and dark circles.)

WE DON'T WANT TO NAG you, BUT WE WILL: EXERCISE IS SO VERY CRITICAL FOR, ALL WOMEN. Regular exercise is critical for your body, to keep your weight regulated and to keep your heart, lungs, and muscles in tip-top shape. It is also critical for your mind. So much of what goes on in our lives as wives and mothers can be emotionally wearying. Regular exercise helps us stay away from that feeling of overload.

GET UP AND GO!

50

A RECENT STUDY IN THE *AMERICAN JOURNAL OF PREVENTIVE MEDICINE* found that three hours of exercise every week could make a significant difference in cases of mild depression. Not only did the subjects feel less depressed, but they kept depression at bay as long as they kept up their exercise routines. So if the thought of exercising to fit into a smaller pair of pants doesn't motivate you, focus instead on the mood-lifting potential and hit the pavement.

With your busy schedule, finding the time to get up and move might require some creativity. Get the kids to come along! Jennifer gets up at the crack of dawn twice a week and runs in the hills with her son's cross-country team. Take it from her: Keeping up with eleven-year-olds is tough!

Walking is one of the best ways to work regular exercise into your life. Lindsay enjoys walking with friends. "It's like meeting for coffee with the bonus of burning calories instead of ingesting them," she says. "Taking a walk with a friend is like a mini therapy session." A quiet walk can give you the mind space to solve a problem, forgive someone, come up with a plan to improve a situation, or just have a cry in peace.

Or make it a family activity and take the kids (and your husband!) along.

You can also sneak in exercise during naptime. Lift weights, do crunches on the ball, jog on a treadmill, get your heart pounding on your exercise bike or elliptical. Pop in an exercise video (have you tried belly dancing) and get moving. There are even groups that show you how you can make your baby a part of your exercise routine. Check online to find one in your community.

RiDiNG HiGh

Did you love horses when you were a little girl? Lots of women did. And now that they are older, they are going back to riding. There is a huge national movement afoot (or astride) of women returning to horses in their forties. They now have the time and the money, and they don't need their parents' permission any longer! Jennifer has joined the horsey trend, riding once a week on a friend's horse and enjoying the strong leg workout that posting can give you. Try it. Perhaps this is your sport!

$\mathcal{A}$ 2-MINUTE MANICURE? Yes, we know that the idea of a "1-minute manicure" is all the rage, but this will take 2 minutes because you'll need to devote 1 minute to stirring the ingredients. You have to work hard for beauty, ladies.

THE 2-MINUTE MANICURE

REMEMBER THE FOOT SCRUB FROM THE VERY beginning of *MomSpa*, MomSpa Indulgence #1, the Lemon Lavender Lift (see page 15)? If you've already mixed that up and used it on your feet, you might have noticed how nice your hands felt afterwards. Spend a little time scrubbing the dead skin off your feet and some of the scrub is bound to get on your hands, isn't it? So why not mix up a similar scrub to use on your hands? You can just use the Lemon Lavender Lift, of course, or you can design something with fewer ingredients that you can mix and use more quickly.

Whaт You'll Need

2-Minute Manicure

¼	cup (70 g) Epsom salts
½	cup (140 g) sea salt
2	ounces (60 ml) apricot kernel oil
10 to 15	drops of your favorite essential oil(s)

Gently mix the salts and apricot kernel oil until well blended. Drop in the essential oils you most enjoy. Using peppermint and basil will help you perk up in the middle of the day, while using calming scents like lavender and chamomile is better if you plan to save your hand treat until the evening is over and you want to wind down.

Apply a small amount to your hands and nails, rubbing the mixture in a circular motion to exfoliate old skin and remove old cuticles. This will also increase circulation. Rinse in warm water and pat dry. If you still feel a bit of oil on your skin, just massage it into your hands, nails, and cuticles until it's absorbed. Use your 2-minute manicure three times a week, and your hands will soon show the difference.

Tнe Real Тнin𝚐

As working moms ourselves, we like to support other working moms. Stay-at-home mom Rosie Herman invented the One-Minute Manicure in order to bring in a bit of extra money. It worked! You can order her product from her Web site at www.oneminutemanicure.com.

Imagine that you could go back in time to a place where you were completely happy.

Think of who you were back then. Were you playing in a band, painting at the ocean, living downtown in a vibrant city, or just hanging out and having fun with your best friends? What if you recreated that time, that person you used to be, and put yourself in a situation to recapture that happy time? Don't worry, we're not suggesting that you change your whole life around and dump your present responsibilities, but what if, what if...what if you built those people, places, and activities into your life again for a few hours once a month?

For Lindsay's fortieth birthday, her husband let her be who she used to be. He took their three young children to his own mother's house for a weekend visit, and Lindsay filled the house with her old friends from high school, blasted out the old eighties rock and roll, left the blender running for hours on end to produce drinks, and floated and giggled in the pool until the stars came out. (Who *wouldn't* giggle at the sight of high school yearbook picture?) For an entire weekend, Lindsay got to be who she used to be— fun, free, and happy.

BE WHO YOU USED TO BE
52

LIFE AS A MOM IS FUN, FREE, AND HAPPY TOO, OF COURSE, BUT IN A much different way! So for a much-deserved indulgent hour or two, think about how you would recapture the best parts of your earlier years. Did you love those late hours in art school, staying up to paint for hours on end? Enroll in a painting class now and get back that part of your life. Were you a mini rock star in your twenties? Strap your guitar back on, drag that drum set up from the basement, and put together another band now! Reconnect with high school friends. Take an evening writing class to reconnect with your studious self.

Our families don't really benefit by our constant suppression of who we really are, and what our real talents and interests are. Let yourself go back and make the time to recapture the best parts. (Please do stick with the *positive* parts of who you used to be, and do not resort to any negative or harmful habits!)

Small Indulgences

Women need to spend time with friends. No matter how busy your life is, carve out the time to just sit and talk with a girlfriend or giggle with a large group of gals. Whether it's a once-a-month book group meeting or a standing invitation to watch *Sex and the City* reruns, your mental health and overall positive attitude depends on it. Never feel guilty about spending time with a friend!

YOUR HOME IS THE CENTER OF YOUR WORLD. No matter how much time you spend away from it, at the office or in the car shuttling children back and forth, home is the center point. And within the home, you need to have an even smaller center for yourself, one that belongs only to you. You deserve privacy and solitude, if only for a few short and precious minutes.

CREATE YOUR OWN SPACE

53

IDEALLY, YOU WOULD HAVE YOUR OWN ROOM, "A ROOM OF ONE'S Own" in the words of Virginia Woolf. A room where everything—the furniture, the colors on the wall, the pillows on the chairs—would reflect your own tastes and the way you want a private sanctuary to look. Alas, few of us really do have rooms of our own. If you can't have a room, take a corner. Or a bathroom, or even just a comfy chair surrounded by your own things.

We all know that it is best to gain by giving, and the best way to get your husband or partner to happily grant you your own territory is to suggest that he deserves some, too! Even allowing the children to each have a spot that they can control will help them respect *your* space. If everyone in the family has his or her own private retreat place, imagine how peaceful it could be!

If you do have a space you can claim, start by painting the walls a calming and soothing color to help you reduce stress the minute you enter and close the door. Find a big comfy chair that will envelop you in its softness on those days you just need to collapse. Fill your space with the scents you love, from candles and incense to bowls of potpourri and fresh fruits.

Build yourself a sacred space within your sanctuary, perhaps a shelf or countertop where you can place selected objects that have great meaning for you. For example, a picture of a place you long to visit will help you focus your thoughts on that and let the stress of the day fall away.

Thε Silεnt Trεatmεnt

Wouldn't a silent vacation be incredible? Just you, in a place with no noise. If you would like to try a contemplative vacation, the monks of Big Sur, California, can help. The New Camaldoli Hermitage Monastery in Big Sur offers single ocean-view rooms and meals to visitors seeking peace in their lives. Visit their Web site at www.contemplation.com for more information. You can learn more about solitude vacations from *Vacations That Can Change Your Life: Adventures, Retreats, and Workshops for the Mind, Body, and Spirit,* by Ellen Lederman.

NEXT TIME YOU HAVE GUACAMOLE ON THE FAMILY DINNER MENU, make a note to treat yourself with an avocado-based hair treatment later that same night. No, this won't actually involve mashing the avocados! Instead, you'll use a very rich avocado oil that will help repair dry and overprocessed hair and treat the hair shaft.

INTENSIVE HAIR TREATMENT

54

PLAN AHEAD

As with any kind of intensive oil treatment for your hair, make sure you don't wait to try the Avocado Oil Hair Repair until the day you have major night-time plans. Oil treatments are good for your hair, no question, but depending on what kind of hair you have, an oil treatment might leave it limp after the first washing. The second time you wash it, the major benefit shines through. So if you plan a big night out with perfectly coiffed hair, you might have unexpectedly limp hair if you treat it the same day. Instead, plan to do 2 or 3 little beauty treatments in the days leading up to your event, which will also allow you to anticipate it that much more!

What You'll Need

Avocado Oil Hair Repair

- 1/4 cup (60 ml) avocado oil
- 3 drops tea tree oil
- 5 drops of your favorite scented oil(s), like lavender, rosemary, or citrus

Mix the ingredients together in a small glass cup. Dip your fingers into the mixture to apply it to your hair. Start with dry (not wet) hair, and begin to work the oil into the bottom ends of your hair where it is driest and most likely to be brittle and split. Massage the ends with the avocado oil mixture. Work your way up the hair strand towards your scalp, dipping your fingers into the mixture and then applying it to your hair. Once you get to your scalp, go ahead and rub the oil into your scalp and give yourself a mini scalp massage. If you have the time, really concentrate on this area—it's so relaxing. Close your eyes and rotate the skin of your scalp with the pads of your fingers, working back down towards the base of your skull. It's a heavenly feeling!

Once you've applied the treatment to your hair, you can wrap your hair first in a plastic bag and then in a towel, to add a bit of warmth and let the oil work really hard. Or you can just wrap a towel around your hair. Leave the treatment on for at least 20 minutes before shampooing it out. Remember to wash your hair by first applying the shampoo to your treated hair, working the shampoo into the hair a bit before adding water. This helps remove more of the oil.

If you have long hair, use the entire recipe in one treatment. If you have medium or short hair, though, one recipe will give you enough for at least two treatments. Store the leftover mixture in a glass bottle and use it for a second application in two weeks.

WE TAKE THE ABILITY TO BREATHE FOR GRANTED. In and out, all day and all night, we draw air into our lungs and send it back out again. But just because we don't spend hours thinking about it, don't underestimate the power of breathing! It can be a tremendous help when it comes to relaxing and de-stressing in a hurry.

BREATHE IN, BREATHE OUT

55

WHAT IS A FREQUENT SIGN OF STRESS? RAPID, SHALLOW BREATHING. Ever notice that when you are in the middle of the grocery store and your children begin to act up, you immediately start to take short little breaths? Pay attention to your breathing the next time this happens, and you will notice it right away. The old advice to "take a deep breath" before responding in anger is a good one, but for our MomSpa purposes, we say take many deep breaths whenever you need them most!

MomSpa Magic

Do you ever wake up still feeling tension from the night before? It's actually very common. Here's a great way to get started in the morning: Loosen your jaw muscles and release tension from your face, neck, and shoulders. Simply open your mouth, place your tongue on the roof of your mouth, and let your jaw become slack. It is an unattractive pose, though, so do this in the privacy of the bathroom!

Here is a simple breathing exercise that can help you feel less stressed:

1. Lie down on the carpet and let your body fall limp.
2. Inhale slowly, and as you inhale, say to yourself, "I am…"
3. Exhale just as slowly and say to yourself, "calm."
4. Repeat your new mantra, "I am calm," along with your slow and steady breathing for several minutes, until you feel a greater sense of ease and are ready to move on to the next part of your day.

We know you can't lie down in the middle of the grocery store aisle to do this exercise during those stressful moments in public, but you can close your eyes for a few seconds and repeat your mantra silently while concentrating on your breathing.

As a way to ensure deep sleep at night (and a way to shut off her "mommy mind"), Jennifer uses focused breathing in bed, quietly listening in her mind to her chant of "calm mind, empty mind" as she tries to eliminate stressful thoughts from her mind. You can make up your own chant—just make sure it's short (one-syllable words to accompany each breath) and that the words encourage ease and a restful mind.

FEELING IN A BIT OF A SLUMP?

Resentful that yet another day of laundry, cooking, and driving awaits you? Here is a fast way to pick yourself up and feel recharged about your home: Move it all around and make something new.

RENEW YOUR HOUSE

56

FOR THOSE OF US ON A BUDGET (AND WE'RE GUESSING THAT'S A LOT of us!), the idea of a major redecorating project is far, far in the future. But as moms, we spend so much time in our own familiar home surroundings that the everyday sameness of the house can make the walls feel like they are closing in…closer…closer… Yikes! Remarkably, just the smallest changes, like moving a picture from one spot to another or rearranging the rugs and side tables, can immediately change the way a room makes you feel.

Jennifer spent a blissful morning recently dragging the furniture around in one small room, trying new combinations of couch over here and armchair over there… and then coffee table here and vase borrowed from the hallway over there. She decided to take things from all over the house and position them in new ways to create a new feeling. Instead of four paintings in four different rooms, she pulled them all off the walls and regrouped them together in her new space. And when she was finished, it was like a new room had been added to her house!

Adding your favorite scented candles and fresh flowers will help you bring that calm spa feeling to your "new" room. So let your chores pile up for an hour or two while you play decorator inside your own house. And then show off your new space to your friends with an afternoon tea party to celebrate.

Deina's favorite wintertime technique to make her house seem suddenly cozier and fresh is to toss orange peels into the fireplace. Mmmm, can you just imagine how great that will smell?

AN AFTERNOON AT THE MALL, BROWSING FROM ONE PLACE TO THE NEXT WITHOUT REALLY INTENDING TO SPEND MONEY. We've all done it, and it does feel like a treat. But imagine this alternative: What if all of those things came to you? You could sit in your favorite chair, mug of coffee in hand, mulling over each thing and trying to imagine how it would fit into your life. (Without ever really meaning to buy it, of course.) But it is still fun to imagine . . .

COFFEE AND A CATALOG

57

YOU CAN MAKE THIS PARTICULAR FANTASY COME TRUE WHENEVER YOU want, thanks to all of the glossy and expensive catalogs that pour into the mailbox. Jennifer likes to save up a stack of catalogs from high-end companies like Tiffany and Company, Neiman Marcus, Gump's, Saks Fifth Avenue, and Horchow, and then devote a quiet afternoon to imaginary shopping.

You can take it one step further in your imagination, if you like: Set yourself a pretend spending limit (a big one, since it's only pretend money) and try to spend it on objects in the catalog. Jennifer's mother used to encourage her to do this to amuse herself on sick days. Then Jennifer's pretend limit was $100; now it is much, much higher!

Travel magazines can serve the same purpose. Decide you are leaving tomorrow on a last-minute jaunt, with money no object. Quick—where are you going? Where will you stay? With a cup of coffee or tea in hand, at ease in your own familiar surroundings, let your mind travel wherever you want.

You could play imaginary spending online, of course, visiting various and sundry Web sites. But it really isn't as much fun as sitting curled up in a comfy chair with a stack of glossy catalogs to thumb through and flag. Turn down the page on that crystal chandelier. Of course you might need it someday!

GROUP ChRISTMAS ShOPPING

A fun evening to plan with your girlfriends is to Christmas-shop together one night without leaving home. Bring all of your catalogs, meet in one cozy home with a bottle of wine and some snacks, and have fun chatting, sharing gift ideas, and swapping catalogs while you pick presents (real ones, not imaginary gifts!) for your family members. Phone in your orders that night and, hey, you are all done with your Santa lists! Now the rest of the month is free, so you can go take in a movie by yourself and claim you were out Christmas shopping.

WE'VE ALREADY GIVEN YOU A FEW RECIPES FOR hAiR TREATMENTS (MomSpa Indulgence #27, Lemon Hair Lust, on page 68, and MomSpa Indulgence #54, Intensive Hair Treatment, on page 120), and we hope you use them often for silky soft strands. However, we realize that there will be days when you just don't have the time to slap on a hair treatment and wait around for 20 or 30 minutes with a towel wrapped elegantly around your head before shampooing thoroughly. In fact, the chance to do something like that in private (because you don't want to give your husband or your children the chance to make a joke at your expense) might not come up very often. So, in the meantime, is there a way to have silky and perfumed hair? There is!

SILKY HAIR EVERY DAY

58

WE ARE RECOMMENDING VERY FEW PRODUCTS IN THIS BOOK, PREFERRING to tell you how to do things on your own. But a product that is well worth purchasing is Biosilk Silk Therapy. Unlike oil-based hair treatments that need to soak in awhile and then shampoo out, Biosilk can be applied to your hair and worn all day long for an amazingly soft, silky feel and a deliciously romantic scent. Just pour a tiny puddle in your palm, rub your hands together, and then run your hands over and through your hair, and you'll immediately smell and feel the difference. It's like a mini-visit to the salon, without having to find a babysitter. You can find Biosilk at many hair salons, or buy it online from www.drugstore.com.

DOES THIS SOUND AT ALL FAMILIAR? You drag
yourself out of bed to face yet another day of driving kids
around and doing the grocery shopping, with a bit of vacu-
uming in between. Why bother to dress up, you think to
yourself, as you pull on the same sweats you wore yesterday. Same time, same to-do list, same old sweats. But
wait—what if those sweats were *hot pink?*

TIME FOR SOME (COLOR) THERAPY

59

WE BELONG TO THE SWEAT SUIT BRIGADE TOO, AND YES, WE CONFESS,
we're seen day after day in the same old comfy outfits. Here is
the MomSpa twist, though: We choose our clothes for their colors. Of course you think about how a particular color will look
on you when shopping and considering any purchase, but do
you ever think about how wearing that color will make you *feel?*
Yes, in addition to perking up your complexion, certain colors
can also literally perk up your mood.

The next time you buy yourself a comfy outfit to schlep
around in, think about these color-therapy qualities and choose
according to your greatest needs:

Pink: Pink soothes and nurtures the wearer and those around her. It dissolves anger and encourages unconditional love.

Red: The color red stimulates the appetite. Perhaps it's not the best color for your workout clothes if weight loss is your goal!

Orange: A warming and energizing color, orange stimulates creativity and encourages fun and sociability.

Yellow: Bright and cheerful, yellow can also be energizing and mood-enhancing.

Green: Jewel tones (jade, teal) and soft blue-greens can be both calming and energizing—and they're flattering to a wide range of skin tones. And if you want to add oomph to your attitude, try a bright chartreuse. But avoid muddy greens like khaki and olive, which can be depressing.

Turquoise: With its cool and calming effect, turquoise is considered good for the immune system in color therapy.

Blue: Blue is calming and relaxing to the wearer, and it's a good healing color.

Indigo Blue: Indigo blue has a sedative effect. This is the one to choose for your most stressful days.

Violet: Also calming for the body and mind, violet is thought to have a purifying effect on the body.

MomSpa Magic

Here is a small color/mood experiment you can try. Focus your attention on something gray for 15 seconds (no, not that ring around your tub—maybe the gray van in front of you at the stoplight). Now, move your eyes over towards something bright and colorful. Don't you feel an immediate lift?

Red is sort of a visual alarm clock. To counteract the dragging sensation that can all too easily sweep over us late in the day, keep a piece of bright-colored clothing around to add to your outfit. A hot pink sweater to slip into, a bright scarf to throw around your neck— anything to keep your mood up and your eyes bright.

THE OLDEST PIECE OF STRESS-BUSTING ADVICE IN THE BOOK IS TO LIE BACK IN A QUIET ROOM, CLOSE YOUR EYES, AND PICTURE A BABBLING BROOK. Uh-huh. Here is how that works for a mom trying to relax this way: You close your eyes and immediately think, *Hey, did I lock the front door? Is the baby monitor on? Did I remember to take the ground beef out to thaw for tonight's burgers?*

When you finally work through all of those panicky thoughts and close your eyes again to picture the babbling brook, your mommy mind takes over again. *Wait! I'm near the water! Where are the kids?* Face it, once you are responsible for a small child, the idea of being near water, *any* kind of water, is far from relaxing. In fact, it is the most stressful thing there is!

DAYDREAMSCAPE

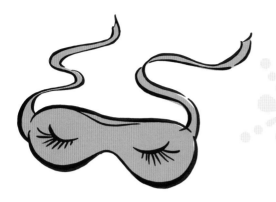

CLOSING YOUR EYES AND MENTALLY FOCUSING ON A MEDITATIVE SCENE really is a good way to relax, though, so we do need to keep it in the MomSpa bag of tricks. But to find the perfect relaxing and stress-free daydreamscape for you to focus on, you will probably have to go through several different scenarios before you hit on the one that lets your tense shoulders unknot.

Jennifer came up with the term *daydreamscape* when she felt the need for a mental vacation. She ran through mental snapshots of years of beach vacations before deciding that they weren't really doing the trick. In fact, the two images that work best for her to focus on during a short daydreamscape are a view of the Eiffel Tower from a hotel window in Paris, and the very physical feeling of horseback riding at a gentle trot. She can close her eyes and let the imagined physical sensation of the horse's movement rock her into a mild meditative state. And she doesn't have to worry about anyone falling off of the horse except her!

Once you've discovered it, you'll be able to go to your private happy place on a regular basis. Having a favorite daydreamscape can come in handy when you are sitting alone in a parking lot, or waiting for the end of soccer practice or the ringing of the school bell. Remember to relax your posture, let your shoulders and your chin drop, close your eyes, and leave today's stress behind.

DEINA HAS SPENT THE PAST 20 YEARS IN THE BEAUTY INDUSTRY AS A DAY SPA OWNER, beauty product developer, and private consultant. You'd think her own beauty regime would be stuffed with high-priced, exclusive products. Well, you'd be wrong. Mostly Deina makes her own simple beauty products by using common ingredients as a basis and adding her own personal twist.

AROMATHERAPY CLEANSERS AND TONERS

CHOOSE AN ESSENTIAL OIL

Depending on your particular skin concern, Deina recommends that you add these essential oils:

Oily or inflamed skin: Add lavender or chamomile oil to the cleanser.

Acne: Add lavender and tea tree oils.

Eczema or psoriasis: Add lavender and cedarwood oils.

Deina likes to use peppermint and eucalyptus in her cleanser to re-energize and "wake up" her skin.

For a high-powered cleanser, Deina has a simple formula:

What You'll Need

Deina's "Secret" Skin-Care Formula

1   bottle Neutrogena cleanser
5   drops essential oil

That's right, just by adding a few drops of your favorite essential oil to an already existing product, you can amp up not only the scent and enjoy the aromatherapy twist, but also add a touch of healing power to it.

After you've customized a cleanser for yourself, why not move on to the toner? "I always use a toner after cleansing, and making my own toner is far more rewarding and healing to my skin," Deina says. Toner is just as simple to make as cleanser.

What You'll Need

Deina's Toner

4   ounces (120 ml) distilled water
5 to 10   drops essential oil

Put these into a spray bottle and shake. Keep the spray bottle handy so that you can give your complexion a boost whenever the mood strikes. "For a real zinger," Deina says, "keep it in the refrigerator so that it is cold when you spray it on!"

What to use? Rose and chamomile oils help soften and hydrate the skin. Keep on spraying!

SURE, YOU TRY TO BE UPBEAT, POSITIVE, AND CHEERFUL THROUGHOUT THE DAY, but let's be honest, you'd have to be Mother Teresa herself not to carry around negativity or anger buried deep inside. Our souls are clouded by negativity, just like black paint added to water. All of us have encountered people, things, and situations that take a negative toll on our emotions.

CLEAR OUT NEGATIVITY

FOR THE MOST PART, WE HAVE THE POWER TO CHOOSE NOT TO ALLOW these factors into our lives. Sometimes that takes planning, and sometimes it takes willpower. Sometimes it takes a great deal of willpower! The thing you need to avoid could be a person, a gambling casino, alcohol, credit cards, junk food, medications, or anything that affects your soul in a negative way.

Lindsay's biggest dose of negativity used to come when she scheduled too many things with her children, which ultimately backfired and left everyone feeling tired and cranky. If she tried to squeeze in just one more errand when it was close to the kids' naptime, she was almost guaranteed an ugly meltdown. Other sources of negativity came from saying "yes" one time too many to volunteer requests, a real problem that all moms face. It all sounds so fun and easy to agree to help out with this and with that, but when you end up staying up late at night to staple together the PTA newsletter at the expense of sleep or relaxation time, it turns into a negative situation. Now that she is aware of the problem, Lindsay works to avoid it.

MomSpa Indulgence #62 sounds simple, but it can make a huge difference to your peace of mind—and your happiness, too. Try this one night when everyone is in bed and the house is quiet: Pour yourself a soothing cup of tea, sit down with a pen and a blank piece of paper, and start to make a list of all of the negative factors in your life, the things that bring you down and cause you stress. Once you have brought these things into focus and written them down, you can start to brainstorm about how to change them.

Make a solid effort to eliminate negative factors from your life. It might be that you have to end an old friendship, or turn down a request for help, or change your eating or exercise habits. It might be as easy as reading the day's news rather than watching it, or switching your radio station. But whether they're easy or hard, it's worth it to make the changes you can. In the end, you will be glad you did.

IN ThE CORNER OF JENNiFER'S OFFiCE, mARKED By a SmaLL RUG, iS AN aREa ThaT LOOKS LiKE a ShRiNE. And it *is* a shrine, of sorts. Not a shrine in the religious sense, but rather a shrine to what she holds dear and understands to be important in her life. It consists of a small low table on which there are pictures of her children and her husband, an old picture of her parents and siblings, small feathers and interesting rocks she picks up on morning walks, and mementos of various travels and journeys. Family, nature, new places. When the day seems to be an endless stream of phone calls and she's feeling overwhelmed by obligations, she can sit near the table and reflect on what is there. (And what is *not* there. What you leave off of your private shrine is just as important as what you put on it.)

CREATE A SACRED SPACE

63

WHAT WOULD YOU PUT IN YOUR SACRED CORNER TO REMIND you of what is important? Yes, you read that right—we did say "corner." Set aside a private corner, not a space in the middle of a room where it would attract too much attention. This is your private sacred space, where you can reflect and feel centered and grounded. Pictures, mementos, natural objects, your children's artwork—it's up to you to decorate your table or shelf with a statement of what means the most to you.

When the world seems out of control and your life seems cluttered by too many other things, refocus on what you hold dear. Remember that life is all about your loved ones, rather than all about the kind of car you drive or the house you live in. Remember that if your house is a mess and your children are getting on your nerves and your husband is late (again), your house, your children, and your husband are *yours*—feel free to relax and rejoice in them.

OUT OF SiGHT

Another way to increase the calmness in your household is to hide whatever gives you stress. Not on a permanent basis, of course, as it does need to be dealt with, but why not gather up your undone work projects, your unpaid bills, and your unanswered letters, and stash them for the weekend? Just clear the decks for one peaceful weekend, so your calm can't be broken by the sight of all that nagging work.

THERE IS NOTHING—NOTHING!—BETTER, THAN A GOOD MASSAGE. We of the MomSpa Team would all love to be able to splurge on weekly massages, but that is far from our reality as hardworking moms-on-budgets!

MASSAGE MANIA

MASSAGE IS EXPENSIVE, AND MONEY CAN BE TIGHT. IN MOMSPA Indulgence #46 (see page 110), we shared the secret of less expensive massage through massage schools, but we also believe you should learn to do it yourself. Many of the adult learning centers around the country have short-session massage lessons that you can take, not so you can become a professional, but just to learn how to give a good massage. Even better, there are couples' massage courses. You both listen, learn, and then practice on each other. Bonus!

For those times when you have to rely on your own basic massage skills instead of those of a high-priced pro, here is Deina's own recipe for a luxurious massage oil.

"I cut a generous handful of lavender—perhaps half a cup— from my lavender plant and add it to an empty glass container," she says. "I shake it down to the bottom, and then cover the lavender cuttings with sesame oil. Then I place the container on the ledge of a sunny window and leave it for a few weeks. I shake it on a daily basis to mix the herbs. After two weeks, I strain the oil to remove the lavender stems. And there you have it, a bottle of your own beautifully scented massage oil!"

Sweet Sheets

As an added benefit, Deina likes to put a little lavender or vanilla fragrance on the sheets, so that when she and her husband Robert have finished massaging each other, they can fall asleep more easily in the soothing scented sheets. What a way to feel pampered at home!

WE STARTED YOU OFF WITH A SIMPLE FOOT
SCRUB, the Lemon Lavender Lift (MomSpa Indulgence #1, see
page 15). Have you tried it yet? If so, you might have thought to
yourself, "Hmmm, what if I rubbed this everywhere? Wouldn't
my skin feel silky and smooth afterwards?" It would indeed,
which is why the same basic recipe can be used to make a full-
body scrub.

BUFFED AND POLISHED

WHEN GIVING YOURSELF A FULL-BODY SCRUB, YOU WILL NEED TO BLOCK
out some time. This is not a process you can sit in the living room
and do like the foot scrub. No, you will need to use your whole
bathroom area, have plenty of warm fluffy towels on hand, and
make sure someone else is going to answer the phone while you
rub and scrub your body with oil.

As the name implies, when you do a full-body scrub, your whole
body will be scrubbed and buffed and polished, one section at a
time. What makes it challenging is that it is a slippery process, and
you need to make sure you don't slip in the tub or shower in the
midst of using all this oil. The safest approach is to sit naked in an
empty tub and, starting at the bottom with your feet, dip your fingers into the scrub and then rub vigorously (not so vigorously that
it hurts or breaks the skin, of course). Spend extra time on your

What You'll Need
Lemon Rose Body Scrub
This is the same basic recipe as for the foot scrub, only doubled. (Your body, you might have noticed, is larger than your feet.)You can replace the rose geranium essential oil with rosemary or lavender if you prefer.

½ cup (150 g) Epsom salts
1 cup (300 g) sea salt
4 ounces (120 ml) apricot kernel oil
20 drops lemon essential oil
20 drops rose geranium essential oil
4 tablespoons chopped lemon zest
6 dried lavender buds, seeds removed from twigs

Mix all of the ingredients in a glass bowl. Apply by scooping out a small amount of scrub at a time and rubbing it over an area with small circular motions.

heels, your elbows, and your feet, the places where your skin is a bit dry and calloused.

The salt scrub is too rough and too oily for the skin on your face, so please stop at your shoulders! But do enjoy scrubbing just about any other part of your exposed skin you can get to. To rinse off, carefully—very carefully—stand and shower, or use a shower hose in the bath. Please be very careful, as the oil will make your tub very slippery. When you have finished this lovely indulgence, you will need to quickly clean the tub so that the next person who uses it doesn't slip and fall either!

Fast Facial
A simple way to buff and polish your face is to pour 2 teaspoons of cornmeal into a bowl, add enough water and then a squirt of lemon juice to make a simple paste, and rub gently over your already cleansed face for a minute. Use gentle rotating circles around your face, avoiding any areas with broken capillaries. Rinse with tepid water and pat dry. Moisturize as usual.

SOMETIMES THE BEST WAY TO RELAX
and unwind is to let your brain do something new
and different. Instead of the same old same old, why
not spend an afternoon creating art or making a
craft project?

CREATIVE CALM

HAVE YOU PICKED UP A PAINTBRUSH SINCE GRADE SCHOOL ART CLASS?
Why not give it a try? Don't focus on whether or not you have
any talent, just focus on how much fun it is to get a paintbrush
wet, dip it into a new pot of paint, and swab your brush
across the paper. The result is not the goal—you don't have to
be da Vinci! The goal is to use your body and your brain in
a whole new way.

Or how about knitting? What could be calmer than 20 minutes with a knitting project? Certainly there is a Zen-like sense
to knitting, to be able to repeat the same motion over and over

again like a physical chant. Quilting can also be Zen-like and restful, as you concentrate on small squares of fabric and perfect tiny stitches instead of your own hectic work schedule or your children's homework. Your brain will enjoy the chance to wander, and your fingers will enjoy the chance to create. Jennifer does needlepoint at night as a way to unwind and detach from the stresses of the household.

When choosing a craft or art project to help you unwind, stick with the simpler sorts. Pottery is lovely, but it requires equipment, glazes, and kilns, and can make a heck of a mess. We don't want you to add stress to your life, but subtract it! Pencil sketching and watercolors are both simple ways to put your creativity to work. They are inexpensive and don't require too much in the way of equipment (particularly with pencil sketches!). You can set your few supplies up and do a quick landscape or portrait on a whim, then quickly put them all away again when you hear your children's footsteps on the path.

Many moms find scrapbooking to be a great way to unwind. Inviting friends over to join you for a night of scrapbooking can result in a fun, hilarious evening, and also knock one more thing off your to-do list (organize last year's Christmas photos)!

IN MomSpa INDULGENCE #59, TIME FOR SOME (COLOR) THERAPY (see page 136), we asked you to consider the effect that different colors have on your mood. Bright colors really do make a difference, don't they? Words can have an equally dramatic effect on your mood. Have you ever started a day in a positive mood, picked up the morning newspaper and read about a terrible tragedy, and felt your mood sink into gloominess? It happens all the time, particularly with all of the bad news that surrounds us nowadays.

POETRY OF THE MIND

WHAT TO DO? OUR PRESCRIPTION IS...POETRY. POETRY? WHAT YOU struggled through in high school? Yes. It is time for you to go back and give poetry a second chance.

Watching fish in an aquarium or stroking the fur of a pet has been shown to lower the heart rate considerably. At MomSpa, we think sitting down and focusing on a poem for a few minutes can achieve the same thing! Reading is, in and of itself, a contemplative thing, but what you read really does affect the way you feel. If you have only a spare 20 minutes to relax, instead of picking up the novel you've been reading, why not read a poem or two by Emily Dickinson? Or the love poems of Pablo Neruda? The beauty of the language, the profundity of the thought, will distract you from your real-life world in a way most novels will not.

Of course, some poetry is serious stuff, and while we certainly approve of you using your brain, we want you to focus right now more on relaxation than mental exertion. Choose a favorite poet or book of poetry that speaks to you or challenges you, but doesn't lead you into subjects like death and despair. Try *The Best American Poetry 2005*, *100 Best-Loved Poems*, or *101 Great American Poems*.

When you feel up to the challenge, why not assign yourself a poem to memorize? Nothing charms a group like someone who can gaze up at the stars and suddenly spout poetry word for word. Why not be that woman?

Be a Journalist

If poetry doesn't appeal to you, why not try journaling? Buy a beautifully bound blank book, sit down with a cup of coffee or tea, and just begin to write. As with the creative arts and crafts projects, don't get hung up on whether what you are writing is any good. The point is just to let your mind wander and to get thoughts down on paper. Set a time limit: For ten minutes, you will write whatever comes to mind without stopping to read and criticize your own work. It's fun!

WhaT KiND OF FOOD REaLLy maKES yoU haPPy? We mean really, *really* happy. Ice cream? Doughnuts? Fresh-out-of-the-oven cookies? In the same way that we moms often deny our need to be pampered and feel guilty when we do indulge ourselves, we also deny the very foods that make us happiest, don't we? Sometimes you've just got to cut loose, and it can be even more fun if you do it by yourself. Because, face it, you don't really want to share that ice cream cone, do you? We thought not!

SPECIAL TREATS FOR YOU

68

WHEN TRAVELING ALONE ON BUSINESS, Jennifer allows herself a hot, gooey Cinnabon at the airport. Calories be damned, these are moments when you need to treat yourself nicely. Not on a weekly basis, or even monthly. But two or three times a year, indulge in the banana split of your dreams. Here's your special treat mantra:

- Ignore calories
- Ignore your budget
- Ignore your weight

It feels good to be restrained, but it feels delicious to break free, to intentionally ignore your own rules on occasion. Be a naughty girl every so often—it does your mind and body good! Schedule it far in advance so that you can daydream about how great that hot cinnamon roll will be, or how tangy the slice of fresh fruit pie will taste, or how cold and rich the newest offering at the ice cream parlor will feel. Focus on how the food will feel in your mouth—creamy soups, gooey desserts.

So go for it—without guilt. Once you've had your little indulgence, you can go back to your regular rigid way of living and eating, safe in your secret knowledge that you've had a tiny splurge, by and golly, you just might do it again sometime!

WE SPEND SO much TimE iN ouR cars, DON'T WE? Running errands, ferrying the children around, commuting to the office. Staying out of the car seems like a treat in itself sometimes. But a car can also help you relax.

DRIVE ON!

DOESN'T IT FEEL COMPLETELY DIFFERENT WHEN YOU ARE DRIVING alone, compared to driving with your backseat filled with children? When the kids are gone, Jennifer cranks up the Black Eyed Peas on her car stereo and shakes her shoulders to the beat. If her boys were in the car, they would all cry out in horror, "Mom, stop that!" and stifle her dancing style. Lindsay drops her girls off at school, opens the sun roof, and rocks out to an old disco tune.

What's the difference? Having no children in your car completely eliminates any interruptions. Kick back and enjoy the alone time: the music you most enjoy, the scenery you can appreciate quietly from the window, the interior temperature you want, and your ability to have a complete thought without distraction.

One mom told us that her favorite thing to do is to get into a freshly washed and waxed car (remember, if you can't take yourself to the spa, take your car!), faintly scented with a touch of lavender spray, and then pop in a smooth jazz CD, sip on a Starbucks iced mocha, and take a long drive to unwind by herself. Ahhh, the all-inclusive-resort possibilities of such a simple thing, taking a quiet drive by yourself!

The car is also a great place to work on improving your posture and tightening those all-important abdominal muscles. Really! Every time you,re stopped at a light or in traffic, hold your head up, put your shoulders back, and lift your diaphragm (the arch of your ribcage). Notice how that pulls in your belly. Soon you,ll be walking taller and leaner!

Makin' Music

Make sure you have a stash of your favorite music close at hand in your car, so that the minute your kids climb out, you can reclaim your territory! No one will complain about the opera you've cranked up, or the jazz you are snapping your fingers to, or the song you slow-danced to in high school. Just you and your music, out for a drive together. Enjoy!

WE MENTIONED THE GLORY OF PEACHES
some pages back, when we suggested the simple beauty
treatment of rubbing peach peels on your face and
then rinsing after 20 minutes or so. Not only do the
fruit acids work wonders, but the smell is heavenly!

PEACHY KEEN

IT'S TRUE—PEACHES ARE A WONDERFUL MILD EXFOLIANT. HERE IS
another way to bring the sweet smell of summer peaches into
your life while the fabulous fruit acids work on removing the
dead skin on your face.

What You'll Need

Peachy Face Treatment

1 ripe peach
¼ cup (60 g) plain yogurt
2 tablespoons (40 g) honey

Peel and slice the peach, add to the yogurt and honey in a blender, and puree on medium for 30 seconds. Apply the mixture to your freshly washed and dried face, and relax in a quiet spot for 15 to 20 minutes. Be sure to breathe deeply to enjoy the scent! Rinse off with warm water.

Small Indulgences

Peaches are also an amazing addition to any busy mom's diet, as they are jammed with cancer-fighting antioxidants like vitamin C and other great vitamins, including vitamin A. Eating peaches is wonderful for your skin, too—they not only improve the health of your skin, but also add color to your complexion. That old phrase "peaches and cream complexion" did have some basis in truth.

When you're planning to treat yourself to a peach face treatment, why not buy double the ingredients and make yourself a healthy fruit bowl for lunch? Peel and slice peaches, add a few blueberries to amp up the antioxidants, and top with a healthy dollop of the very same plain yogurt you plan to use on your face in a few minutes.

IS THERE ANYTHING MORE PEACEFUL THAN A CUP OF TEA? Coffee is sheer heaven, of course, and we moms all thrive on it. But tea . . . tea just seems so much calmer, doesn't it? Turns out the caffeine levels really aren't that different, but a cup of tea just exudes peace and quiet in a way that coffee symbolizes hustle and bustle. In fact, dedicated tea drinkers believe that when we're feeling down and depressed, tea has a way of soothing and comforting. At the very same time though, when you're feeling excited, tea has a way of calming you down. How lucky we are to have such a versatile brew at our fingertips!

A QUIET CUP OF TEA

MAKE THE TIME AND EFFORT TO SET ASIDE THE HUSTLE AND BUSTLE, then, for a quiet cup of tea. There is much more ritual in tea drinking than coffee drinking anyway, and you can surrender yourself to the flow of your own tea ceremony.

The Legend of Tea

Ever wonder how people started drinking tea? The legend surrounding the beginnings of tea is that a Chinese emperor was relaxing in his garden with a mug of hot water when a few leaves from a nearby tree floated down and landed in his cup. Lucky for us, right?

You don't need to commit yourself to any one type of tea—develop a selection of teas for a variety of reasons. Perhaps an expensive Chinese tea like smoky Lapsang Souchong to share with visitors, an herbal sleep-inducing tea to help you unwind, and the traditional Earl Grey for mid-morning breaks.

If you find it hard to shut off your busy brain and relax while sitting down for just a few minutes, why not use your cup of tea for a small meditation technique? Close your eyes and picture where the tea in your cup came from. Picture a tea plantation in a land far, far away. Try to hear the sounds of that country, try to smell the smells. Reflect on how far those tea leaves have traveled to make it into your cup this morning. It will remind you that you are a critical part of the big, wide world.

Although Jennifer is a black-coffee drinker through and through, she drinks her tea with milk and sugar. Nothing like a milky cup of sweet tea to make you feel like the Queen of England on an ordinary day.

Small Indulgences

No matter how much you enjoy your cup of tea, chances are you aren't nearly as devoted as the folks at www.nicecupofteaandasitdown.com. In addition to creating a Web site worth visiting, these charming folks have written the book on how important it is to stop, pour a cup of tea, and sit down for a few minutes.

WE THINK THERE IS NO END TO WHAT YOU CAN DO IN A BATHTUB...REALLY!

We've shared several different recipes for bath salt soaks (see MomSpa Indulgences #45 and #65 on pages 108 and 148). Now it is time to move on to silky smooth bath oil.

ORGASMIC ORANGE

IMAGINE THIS: YOU LIE BACK IN A hot tub, eyes closed as you breathe in the scents of the citrus grove around you... Sound good? We can't bring you a whole citrus grove (and that sounds a bit dirty anyway—all that soil on the roots!), but we can help you bring that sharp, intoxicating scent to life.

What You'll Need

Orange Bath Oil

1 fresh orange
2 tablespoons (28 ml) almond oil
10 drops citrus essential oil

Slice the unpeeled orange into very thin round slices. Mix the oils in a small cup or bowl. Run a hot bath and add the oils. Float the orange slices in the water, and insert self into tub. Close your eyes, breathe deeply, and let your mind wander to whatever exotic scene most appeals.

Small Indulgences

Oranges aren't just good for your bathtub. German researchers found that high doses of vitamin C helped combat feelings of stress. And vitamin C is critical to your body's health and vitality—both for promoting collagen production and for providing a healthy luster to your hair, skin, and nails. So ramp up your vitamin C intake whenever you can. In addition to oranges, strawberries, broccoli, cantaloupe, and tomatoes are all excellent sources that you and your family can enjoy.

JENNIFER IS A BIG FAN OF MARTINIS. Okay, make that a *huge* fan of martinis. In fact, she wrote a whole book about them called *The Martini Diet*, about an indulgent approach to weight loss. (Really!) But you can't drink martinis all day long now, can you? It tends to interfere with effective parenting. So the MomSpa approach is to make yourself a body splash with a fun martini twist!

THE BIG SPLASH

73

JENNIFER'S OWN PERSONAL MARTINI IS GinSander, the basis for this body splash. A GinSander is a dry gin martini with a twist of lemon and a sprig of lavender, and it's the perfect summertime martini. She uses the same scents and tastes to create a body splash to invigorate her skin whenever she needs a quick pick-up. Sounds nutty, yes, to splash gin on your skin, but alcohol really is the basis for all toners and splashes.

MomSpa Magic

Jennifer created her own recipe based on her favorite drink and gives this body splash away as a custom-made gift for friends. Why not invent your own custom blend of this or any of the MomSpa recipes and use those as special gifts?

If you are a Cosmo fan, you can of course modify this recipe to give it a sweeter air simply by choosing essential oils that better mimic the fruity scents of one of those cocktails.

What You'll Need
GinSander Body Splash

$1/2$ ounce (15 ml) cider vinegar
$1/8$ ounce gin (use a cheaper brand, please, not your very best!)
5 ounces (150 ml) distilled water
3 drops lavender essential oil
5 drops lemon essential oil

Mix the ingredients together and store in a glass jar in the fridge. Give your face or body a quick splash with this water whenever you feel run down. Take a deep breath, let those essential oils perk you up, and focus on the martini you could soon be having with your friends!

ON hER TREASURED VISITS TO THE RITZ-
CARLTON SPA AT HALF MOON BAY, Jennifer longed
to take home a little something other than a new attitude and
the thrill of being pampered. She was after spa secrets that she
could do at home.

TOUCH OF THE RITZ

AFTER APPLYING A BIT OF GENTLE PRESSURE, JENNIFER PERSUADED THE
talented ladies and gentlemen who work in the spa to offer up
their own favorite at-home treatments! Close your eyes while
you do them and try to picture yourself in an elegant spa...

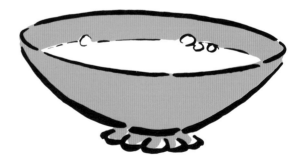

What You'll Need
Toning Milk Bath

1	cup (290 g) sea salts
2	cups (150 g) powdered milk
$\frac{1}{2}$	tablespoons baking soda
$\frac{1}{2}$	tablespoons cornstarch
5 to 8	drops lavender essential oil, or any oil with your favorite scent

Combine all of the ingredients in a bowl and pour into the running water of a hot tub. Soak and enjoy this toning and soothing milk bath.

What You'll Need
Almond Citrus Scrub

$\frac{1}{2}$	cup (40 g) orange, grapefruit, or lemon zest (use in combination or individually)
$\frac{1}{2}$	cup (50 g) almonds
$\frac{1}{3}$	cup (100 g) sea salts

1 tablespoon (15 ml) almond oil

Combine the zest and almonds in a blender. Blend until the mixture is a fine powder. Mix the powder together with the sea salts and almond oil. Use on your body for exfoliation, scooping up a bit of the scrub with your fingers and rubbing it on your skin in small circular motions. Rinse off with warm water.

WE hOPE yOU'VE ENJOyED ThE PREVioUS 74 wayS TO PamPER yoUR miND, BODy, aND SPiRiT here in *MomSpa*. But you won't truly enjoy any of them until you adopt MomSpa Indulgence #75 as your slogan. Please give up the guilt for good, the guilt over taking the time to take care of yourself. The guilt over spending time and attention on your own needs. The guilt over the occasional splurge that makes you happy.

GIVE UP THE GUILT!

REMEMBER THE MOMSPA CREDO:

You deserve to have time to yourself on a regular basis.

You deserve to spend money from the family budget on beauty and pampering treats.

You deserve the right to declare a small corner of the house yours and yours alone.

You deserve to unwind and recharge yourself as often as needed.

You deserve all of these, and more. The happier and less stressed *you* are, the happier your family life will be. In a day when even British Airways advertises "spa services" as a way of standing out in a crowded travel field, we hope to someday see a world in which enterprising massage therapists set up tables alongside the soccer fields on Saturday mornings, manicurists pop up in the meat department of the grocery store, and you can get a bikini wax while your oil is being changed. Will that happen? Not likely. But the more vocal you are about your need to feel special, to unwind, to spend some time *alone* on occasion, the easier it will become.

It can be hard to speak up and say you need some time (or some money) for yourself. Be gentle, but firm. Speak up about your own needs and point out how great the benefit to everyone will be once you are no longer a quivering bundle of nerves.

Remember, spending time and money on yourself does not make you a bad mom. It doesn't make you a bad wife or partner. It makes you a strong, happy, and relaxed person who takes joy in the world around her.

MomSpa Magic

Plant your garden full of MomSpa mother's helpers: rosemary, lavender, sage, lemon balm, basil, mint. Try growing lemon, lime, and orange trees in pots around your garden. Citrus flowers are wonderfully scented, and the fruits smell and taste heavenly and are filled with stress-busting vitamin C!

Small Indulgences

Make the most of small moments. Deina even uses time outdoors with her kids to pause, break off a bit of rosemary growing in her backyard, and roll it back and forth in her hands. She takes a deep breath of rosemary to energize herself, and then keeps the piece in her pocket to use for another quick burst of energy whenever she needs it.

Quick

PICK-UPS,
RECIPES, AND
RESOURCES

Relax, Rejuvenate, Restore—In Minutes!

SUGGESTIONS FOR QUICK PICK-UPS

If your time is as limited as ours, you need to make the most of every minute. So here's an at-a-glance guide to choosing MomSpa Indulgences from our list of 75, based on how much time you have to enjoy them.

15 Minutes

If you can grab a quick 15 minutes to yourself, here are a few simple ways to spend the time for maximum benefit.

#2 Shoulder Drops and Neck Rolls (page 18)
With just a few minutes, you can stretch and unwind tension from your upper body.

#36 Love Notes to You! (page 88)
Spend a few minutes writing an encouraging note to yourself.

#48 Early Morning in the Garden (page 114)
Even 15 minutes standing peacefully in the stillness of the morning can help center you for the day ahead.

#58 Silky Hair Every Day (page 134)
Just squirting Biosilk Silk Therapy, or running a perfume advertising strip over your hair, will give you a glamorous scent all day long.

#60 Daydreamscape (page 138)
Take a 15-minute trip to another place with a daydreamscape.

#73 The Big Splash (page 164)
Once you've made this simple body tonic, you can splash it on any time you need a pick-me-up.

1 Hour

One whole hour! How will you spend it? Why not try one of these ideas:

#7 Japanese Retreat (page 28)
Seek out the calmness of a Japanese restaurant and feel like you are a world away.

#10 Ten Things You Love (page 34)
Once you've drawn up your list, devote a free hour to making sure you do at least one of them!

#16 Catch a Catnap (page 46)
It will take a few weeks to really train your body to take a quick catnap, but once you can do it, it is positively addictive.

#21 The Morning Market (page 56)
Spend a pleasant hour at a local farmers' market buying fresh seasonal organic produce and connecting with the folks who grow your food.

#31 Play Dress-Up (page 76)
With an hour to spend, you can dive into your closet and have fun with a bout of dress-up to discover new outfits or anticipate an upcoming event.

#71 A Quiet Cup of Tea (page 160)
Select the tea that matches your mood, put the kettle on, sit quietly, and enjoy!

3 Hours

Wow! Three hours? A delicious treat for any busy mom. With three hours, you can really unwind and pamper yourself in so many ways, including:

#5 Instant Getaway (page 24)
Pull out your already packed bag of pampering tricks and choose your favorites!

#12 Stop and Smell Someone Else's Roses (page 38)
Seek out the quiet calm of a public garden, and don't be surprised if you can wonder alone and imagine it's your dream garden.

#22 Glamour on the Cheap (page 58)
Round up your old makeup and head to the mall to learn new ways to apply it from professional makeup artists.

#43 Send in the Maids! (page 104)
Arrange for a one-time housecleaning service, or plan your garage sale now and dedicate the proceeds to hiring some help.

#63 Create a Sacred Space (page 144)
Spend three hours choosing and arranging the objects that mean so much to you into a small shrine to focus on during the day.

#66 Creative Calm (page 150)
Pull out the paper and paint and get busy letting your inner artist emerge. Don't hold back, don't focus on talent, just let your creative juices flow!

The MomSpa WEEKEND

A little Mozart in the air, a lot of scented candles, a fuzzy terry cloth robe emblazoned with a fancy crest, your feet scrubbed smooth and soaking in a hot tub of water... Must be some fancy spa, eh? Alas, no. It could be your house, though, on a Saturday when, in a lovely twist of fate, your family has gone for the weekend and left you behind.

WELCOME TO THE MOMSPA WEEKEND, WHERE BEING PAMPERED AND indulged can take a whole two days!

Total bliss, a weekend to yourself! Even if you spent the whole time on the couch reading back issues of Oprah's magazine and ordering in pizza, it would be a grand two days.

With your newly adopted MomSpa attitude, though, you can turn those precious two days into a time to relax, renew, and rejuvenate. By the time your family returns on Sunday night, they will be greeted at the front door by a whole new woman!

First, set the stage by following MomSpa Indulgence #39 (page 94) and making a crystal pitcher of water filled with ice and citrus slices for that you-are-really-in-a-spa touch. You might also want to add to the atmosphere with MomSpa Indulgence #3 (page 20), and fill your rooms with scented steam using a vaporizer. Why not also go shopping for a special new music CD like in MomSpa Indulgence #19 (page 52) that will help the weekend sound special and take you on a musical vacation?

Saturday

It's your first day at our MomSpa Weekend. Let's get started—we know you don't want to waste a minute!

MORNING

Good morning! Start your spa weekend off with a mild warm-up with exercise (MomSpa Indulgence #50, page 118) in the form of a long, quiet walk.

Once you've returned from your walk, take some time to do shoulder drops and neck rolls (MomSpa Indulgence #2, page 18) to release tension.

When your body is relaxed, lie on the carpet and practice breathing exercises (MomSpa Indulgence #55, page 128).

Make sure to drink water from your pitcher throughout the day.

Okay, your body and your mind are now tension-free (or at least less tense than when you started!). Why not spend an hour or more rearranging your furniture to give your house a new look (MomSpa Indulgence #56, page 130)? Take advantage of the fact that no one else is there to offer an opinion or objection. Even if you have to put it all back when your family returns, you can at least have a few short days of a house with a changed look.

Find a massage school in your area that offers inexpensive

massages by their students (MomSpa Indulgence #46, page 110) and indulge in an entire hour of bliss.

Return home and—gasp—take a catnap! MomSpa Indulgence #16 (page 46) has suggestions on how to train your body to fall asleep quickly.

After a lovely little nap, why not pour yourself a cup of tea, sit in your newly arranged living room, and draw up your list of the ten things you love (MomSpa Indulgence #10, page 34). Is there anything on the list that you still have time to do today?

EVENING

Make sure you indulge your own personal taste at dinner (MomSpa Indulgence #24, page 62) since you don't have to worry about who likes what. Try some of the luscious MomSpa recipes starting on page 180 and enjoy!

Go ahead and get beautiful in a messy kind of way—with a simple facial like the Milk and Honey Mask (MomSpa Indulgence #42, page 100) and a Lemon Lavender Lift foot scrub (MomSpa Indulgence #1, page 15). You can sit in your own house without worrying that your husband and children will make fun of the fact you have stuff on your face.

And since you are alone…indulge in several hours of a good weepy girl movie (MomSpa Indulgence #33, page 82) that will help you clear out whatever tension you have left!

You don't *have* to be alone, of course—this is a great excuse to round up your girlfriends and have a spa party (MomSpa Indulgence #14, page 42) of your own!

Sunday

Another whole day just for you (or you and your friends). Here are some suggestions on how to spend it.

MORNING

Day number two of quiet bliss! Why not start your day early and watch the sun rise in your garden (MomSpa Indulgence #48, page 114), sitting in your very own outdoor retreat (MomSpa Indulgence #44, page 106).

Wake your face up with icy toner pads (MomSpa Indulgence #35, page 86) to eliminate that morning puffiness.

Take an aromatherapy shower (MomSpa Indulgence #20, page 54) to set the tone for your day. Scent the washcloth with peppermint or lemons to perk yourself up.

Once you are showered and wrapped in a thick robe, sit down and practice a little forgiveness (MomSpa Indulgence #17, page 48) to clear your mind and lighten your emotions. Get it all down on paper, and bury that letter nice and deep!

The More, the Merrier.

Invite another mom to join you on your MomSpa weekend. Together, you can split the cost of ingredients like essential oils and both benefit from the good company and the savings for your budgets.

With a clear heart, set to work making a sacred space for yourself (MomSpa Indulgence #63, page 144) where you can reflect and honor what is most important to you.

SmALL INDULGENCES
Plug in your bread machine and make a fresh loaf. The smell of baking bread will add to your sense of relaxation, and the delicious bread will be great at your next meal!

EVENING

Get to work on your body with a thorough body scrub (MomSpa Indulgence #65, page 148) that will leave your skin soft and silky.

At the same time, you can put an intensive hair treatment (MomSpa Indulgence #54, page 126) in your hair to work its magic. Remember, though, never do an oil treatment on your hair if you have big evening plans. It might be limp after washing.

Make a simple plan for dinner (MomSpa Indulgence #40, page 96) in case you are expecting to feed your family that night. If not, seek out the peace of a Japanese restaurant (MomSpa Indulgence #7, page 28) and absorb the calm there.

See how much you can accomplish for your body, mind, and spirit in just two short days? Now that you have 75 different MomSpa Indulgences at your fingertips, you can mix and match them to suit your needs. There will be times when all you want is a full day of beauty treatments. And there will be times when you need to focus on clearing your mind and connecting with your spirit.

MomSpa Recipes

Sure, we've heard that old saying, "nothing tastes as good as being thin," but come on... Is that the way you want to live when you finally get the chance to pamper yourself? We thought not.

A SPA EXPERIENCE IS ABOUT SO MUCH MORE THAN LOSING WEIGHT nowadays, and some of the poshest spas now have the fanciest menus. No carrot sticks when you are paying hundreds of dollars a day. So when you are designing your own spa meals, cut yourself some slack.

Some of our recipes are decadent, true, and all of them are delicious. Some are certainly low-calorie, but rather than focusing on their caloric content, instead we suggest monitoring your portion size. Not only does that automatically limit the calories you'll take in, but it also adds to the spa feeling because you won't overeat and end up feeling heavy and filled up.

Enjoy our MomSpa recipes by mixing and matching starters, main dishes, and—of course!—desserts, to make light meals to enjoy by yourself or with others.

Soups and Salads

Sweet Potato Soup

This is Jennifer's favorite way of giving her body a huge dose of vitamin A. It is wonderful served warm on a cold day, or served cold on a hot day!

Ingredients
- $1/2$ cup (65 g) peeled and chopped yellow onion
- 3 tablespoons (40 g) butter
- 4 cups (950 ml) chicken stock
- 1 cup (235 ml) very sweet white wine (like a Riesling)
- 2 or 3 large sweet potatoes, peeled and cut into chunks
- Salt and pepper

Sauté the onion in the butter in a large soup pot until soft and beginning to brown. Add the stock, wine, sweet potatoes, and salt and pepper to taste and bring to a gentle boil. Reduce the heat and simmer until the sweet potatoes can be pierced easily with a knife. Remove from heat and allow to cool for 10 to 15 minutes. Process soup in a blender or food processor until creamy and smooth. Adjust seasonings to taste. **Serves 6.**

Pear and Pecan Salad

Perfect for an autumn afternoon, when you have spent the morning at the farmers' market buying fruit, nuts, and honey direct from the growers.

Ingredients
- $3/4$ cup (185 g) plain yogurt
- 3 tablespoons (60 g) fresh honey
- 3 tablespoons (45 ml) lemon juice
- Freshly ground black pepper
- 1 bag mixed salad greens (choose one that contains radicchio)
- 2 ripe pears, peeled and sliced
- $1/2$ cup (75 g) dried cherries or cranberries
- $1/2$ cup (65 g) chopped pecans

Make a salad dressing by combining the yogurt, honey, lemon juice, and pepper to taste. Mix all other ingredients in a salad bowl, pour the dressing over, and toss to coat. **Serves 6.**

Gazpacho

The quintessential cold summer soup, very spa-like in presentation and flavors! Also a wonderful way to use the fresh vegetables you just picked up at your morning foray to the farmers' market.

Ingredients
  2 medium tomatoes, peeled and cut into chunks
  ½ cucumber, peeled and cut into chunks (not slices)
  ¼ red bell pepper, seeded and cut into chunks
  2 small cloves garlic
  2 tablespoons (8 g) fresh parsley
  4 teaspoons (20 ml) red wine vinegar
  1 cup (235 ml) tomato juice
Salt and pepper

Place the tomatoes, cucumber, bell pepper, garlic, and parsley in a blender or food processor. Blend or process until well mixed but still chunky (not a puree). Stir in the vinegar and tomato juice. Place the bowl of the blender or processor in the refrigerator for at least 2 hours before serving. Taste before adding salt and pepper to your liking. To turn this into a quick simple supper, grill a few shrimp and put them on top of the gazpacho. **Serves 2.**

Panzanella (Tuscan Tomato and Bread Salad)

This hearty, satisfying salad makes a wonderful summer lunch.

Ingredients
  6 cups (210 g) fresh French bread, torn or cut into small cubes
  3 tomatoes, cut into wedges
  3 slices red onion, quartered
  3 tablespoons (8 g) fresh basil, torn into small pieces
  ¼ cup (55 g) extra-virgin olive oil
  3 tablespoons (45 ml) white wine vinegar
Salt and pepper

Preheat the oven to 450°F (230°C, or gas mark 8) and place the torn bread cubes on a baking sheet. Toast for 5 to 10 minutes, until golden brown. (Every few minutes, open the oven and shake the pan to toast all sides.) Let the croutons cool. In a large salad bowl, toss together the tomatoes, croutons, onion, and basil. Whisk together the olive oil and vinegar, drizzle over the salad, and toss to mix. Taste and add salt and pepper as needed. **Serves 6.**

Simple Corn Chowder.

This is a soothing and easy summer soup if you use fresh corn in season, but you can treat yourself to it all year long by substituting frozen corn. Experiment by using heavy cream, adding more bacon and potatoes, and turning it into a hearty soup for winter.

Ingredients
6   ears fresh sweet corn
6   cups (1,425 ml) chicken stock
3   cloves garlic, peeled, smashed, and chopped
3   small red potatoes, cut into chunks (leave peel on)
5   slices bacon, cut into small pieces
1   medium yellow onion, chopped
2   cups (475 ml) milk
1   cup (155 g) cherry tomatoes, each cut in half

Using a table knife, cut the corn off the cobs and set aside. In a large soup pot, mix the stock, garlic, and corn cobs and simmer for 10 minutes. Remove cobs. Add the potatoes and half of the fresh corn to the broth. Simmer until the potatoes are tender. Remove from the heat and allow to cool for 10 minutes. While the soup is cooling, cook the bacon and onion together in a frying pan until the bacon is almost crisp. Remove from the heat. Puree the soup, and put it back into the soup pot. Add the milk, the rest of the corn, the bacon, onion, and as much of the cooking fat from the bacon as desired. Simmer for 10 minutes. Remove from the heat. Add the tomatoes, stir, and serve. **Serves 6.**

CURRIED ORANGE PUMPKIN SOUP

Seek out a sweet pumpkin like Cinderella, Spookie, or other type of sugar pumpkin. You can also use canned pumpkin in a pinch, but the flavor isn't as smooth. Be warned that it takes at least half an hour to cut up the pumpkin and remove the rind (which Jennifer did not know the first time she tried to make this).

Ingredients
- 2 tablespoons (28 g) extra-virgin olive oil
- 1 tablespoon (15 g) butter
- 1 onion, peeled and chopped
- 5 cups (1,140 ml) chicken stock
- 1 five-pound (2.25 kg) sweet pumpkin, cut, chopped, and seeded so that you are left with just the cubed flesh (about 4 cups worth)
- 2 russet potatoes, peeled and cubed
- 1 tablespoon orange zest
- $^1/_2$ teaspoons curry powder (or more to taste)
- Salt and pepper
- $^3/_4$ cup (175 ml) heavy cream

In a large soup pot, mix the olive oil, butter, and onion. Sauté until the onion begins to brown. Add the stock, pumpkin, and potatoes to the soup pot and bring to a boil. Turn down the heat and simmer until the potatoes and pumpkin are both tender when pierced, about 20 minutes. Remove from the heat and allow to cool for 10 minutes. Using a blender or food processor, puree until smooth. Return to the soup pot and add the zest and curry powder. Stir and taste to adjust seasonings. You might want to add a bit more curry powder or even more orange zest, as well as the salt and pepper. Just before serving, pour in the cream and stir gently (taste and adjust the seasonings again to make sure the cream hasn't dampened the flavor). **Serves 6.**

Main Dishes

Sweet Chicken and Vegetables

This simple and light dish is easy to make, and your house will smell heavenly. The broth is also heavenly, and best spooned over basmati rice. Jennifer developed this recipe over years of trying to do something interesting with chicken thighs and also with what grows in her garden.

Ingredients

2 tablespoons (28 g) olive oil
½ yellow onion, peeled and chopped
2 tablespoons fresh sage, rinsed and torn into small pieces
6 chicken thighs, skin left on
1 cup (235 ml) sweet white wine
½ cup (120 ml) water
1 cup (130 g) baby carrots
1 cup (110 g) fresh green beans
Salt and pepper

Preheat the oven to 325°F (170°C, or gas mark 3). In a large ovenproof soup pot with a lid, mix the olive oil, onion, and sage. Cook over medium heat for 5 minutes, stirring frequently. Add the chicken thighs and cook, turning until browned on both sides. Once the chicken is well browned, pour in the wine and water and bring to a boil. Remove from the stovetop and cover. Place in the oven and cook for 15 minutes. Add the carrots and the green beans. (Be careful when removing the lid, as steam will escape.) Shake the pot to get the vegetables down into the liquid. Cover, and continue baking for another 20 minutes. Add salt and pepper to taste. **Serves 6.**

GRILLED SALMON PACKETS

This sounds like a campfire meal, and it is! You can make this when out camping with your family, but you can also do it the way Lindsay does—invite some girl-friends over, start up the grill, pour some wine, and when your first glass is done, your dinner is, too!

Ingredients
2 salmon steaks
½ yellow onion, peeled and sliced thinly
1 yellow squash, sliced thinly
1 zucchini, sliced thinly
3 tablespoons (42 g) extra-virgin olive oil
Black pepper
Garlic salt

Preheat the grill. With heavy-duty aluminum foil, make yourself two double-strength aluminum packets. Place the salmon steaks in the center and place the vegetables around them. Drizzle with the olive oil, add pepper and garlic salt to taste, and seal up the salmon packets. Place on the hot grill. Cook for 10 to 20 minutes, checking doneness after 10 minutes. (Cooking time varies depending on the thickness of the fish and the heat of the grill.) This can also be cooked around the coals of a campfire. **Serves 2.**

SAUTÉED LEMON SOLE

Not everyone likes the fishy smell of sole, but for those who do, this is a light, simple, flavorful supper to make for yourself.

Ingredients
4 sole fillets, rolled
¼ cup (60 ml) sweet white wine
1 lemon, sliced very thinly (remove seeds but leave the rind on)
2 tablespoons (28 g) butter
3 tablespoons (45 ml) fresh lemon juice
Salt and pepper

In a saucepan with a lid, place the rolled sole and pour the wine over it. Add half of the lemon slices to the broth around the fish. Bring to a gentle boil, turn the heat down, cover, and simmer for 3 minutes. Check doneness (the fish loses its pinkness), and cook for another minute if needed. Gently remove the fish and set aside. Bring the liquid left in the pan to a boil and cook until reduced by half. Add the butter and lemon juice, and whisk until smooth. Place two fillets on each plate and pour the sauce over them. Add salt and pepper to taste. Decorate with the remaining lemon slices. **Serves 2.**

HEALThy GARDEN BakE

For those of us with abundant summer gardens, a recipe that uses everything we grow is a handy thing to have. Lindsay developed this tasty recipe for a light vegetarian meal.

Ingredients
1   eggplant, sliced thinly
2   zucchini, sliced thinly
1   large yellow onion, peeled and sliced thinly
1   cup (235 ml) balsamic vinegar
½   cup (55 g) sun-dried tomatoes packed in oil, cut into small pieces
3   tablespoons (45 ml) oil from sun-dried tomatoes
1   cup (80 g) Parmesan cheese, shredded

Place all of the sliced vegetables into a gallon-size resealable plastic bag. Pour in the balsamic vinegar. Zip shut and refrigerate overnight to marinate. When ready to bake, preheat the oven to 350°F (180°C, or gas mark 4) and spread the veggies and any remaining liquid on a large baking sheet with a rim. Sprinkle the sun-dried tomatoes on top, and then drizzle the oil all over the veggies. Bake for 45 minutes. Remove from the oven and spread the cheese over the top. Place back in the oven until the cheese is melted. This is wonderful served with basmati rice. You can also add extra-firm tofu to the veggie mixture for more protein. **Serves 2.**

Lemon and Garlic Shrimp

The taste of fresh lemons and fresh shrimp is the taste of summer! Your kitchen will smell divine with these ingredients on the stove.

Ingredients
- 5 tablespoons (75 ml) extra-virgin olive oil
- 3 large cloves garlic, peeled, smashed, and chopped
- 2 tablespoons (8 g) fresh parsley
- 3 tablespoons (45 ml) fresh lemon juice
- 1/4 pound (340 g) medium shrimp, shelled and deveined

Mix the olive oil, garlic, parsley, and lemon juice in a bowl. Add the shrimp and allow to marinate for at least 30 minutes. Heat a sauté pan and, holding back the shrimp, pour the oil mixture in. Allow to heat for 1 minute, then add the shrimp and cook quickly for a few minutes until they turn white. Serve with rice or fresh pasta. **Serves 2.**

Crispy Salmon

Like Lindsay, Deina is a salmon lover. Her favorite MomSpa indulgence is this comfort-food fave using potato chips! Your children might even eat their fish if you cook it this way.

Ingredients
- 1 cup (250 g) crushed potato chips
- 2 salmon steaks
- 2 tablespoons (30 ml) olive oil

Preheat the oven to 350°F (180°C, or gas mark 4). Place the crushed chips in a large bowl, and dip the salmon steaks to coat evenly. Pour the olive oil into a glass baking pan and place the steaks in the pan. Bake for 10 minutes. Check for doneness. Continue baking until salmon reaches desired doneness. **Serves 2.**

Desserts and Smoothies

Berry Doodle

Jennifer invented this simple dessert while pregnant and running late on the food for a dinner party.

Ingredients
2 freshly baked snickerdoodle cookies
1 cup (120 g) fresh berries (strawberries, blueberries, blackberries)
1 tablespoon brown sugar
⅓ cup (75 g) sour cream

Place a cookie on each plate and mound fresh berries on top. Mix the brown sugar and sour cream together in a small dish, and garnish the berries with a healthy dollop. Enjoy! **Serves 2.**

Lindsay's Breakfast Smoothie

Lindsay starts her days with a super-nutritious smoothie. It's a major antioxidant jolt.

Ingredients
6 ounces (175 ml) soymilk (Lindsay likes Silk)
1 scoop Juice Plus Vanilla Complete*
1 tablespoon blueberries
1 tablespoon flaxseed
1 tablespoon brewer's yeast
1 tablespoon green tea leaves
¼ fresh banana

Put all the ingredients into a blender and blend until smooth. Drink up! **Serves 1.**

*Order information can be found in the resource section on page 192.

OLiVE OiL CakE

This is a wonderfully light summer cake from Italy's Tuscan region.

Ingredients

  5 eggs, separated
  2/3 cup (135 g) sugar
  2 teaspoons finely minced fresh rosemary
Grated zest of one lemon and one orange
  4 ounces (65 g) fresh ricotta cheese
  1/2 cup (110 g) extra-virgin olive oil
  1/4 cup (60 ml) late-harvest white wine (very sweet dessert wine)
  1/2 cups (175 g) flour
  1/4 teaspoon salt

Preheat the oven to 350°F (180°C, or gas mark 4). In a large bowl, beat the yolks with the sugar until they are pale yellow in color. Fold in the rosemary and the zests and set aside. In another bowl, beat together the ricotta, oil, and wine. Mix the flour and salt together and add to the egg/sugar mixture, alternating with the ricotta mixture, in 3 doses. Stir gently in between. In another bowl, beat the egg whites until stiff. Fold into the batter. Pour into an ungreased 10-inch (25-cm) springform pan and bake for 25 minutes. Then turn down the heat to 325°F (170°C, or gas mark 3) and cook an additional 20 minutes. Cool the cake completely before unmolding. **Serves 6.**

RoaSTED PEaChES

Every woman should know how to roast fruit. Really. It is a simple and somewhat healthy dessert that will impress guests and make you feel special when dining alone.

Ingredients

2 tablespoons (28 g) butter
2 peaches, cut in half and pits removed
1 tablespoon brown sugar

Preheat the oven to 400°F (200°C, or gas mark 6). Add the butter to a glass baking dish and set in the hot oven for 3 minutes, until melted. Place the peaches cut side down in the butter. Roast until tender, about 15 minutes. Remove from the oven and turn the peaches in the dish so that the cut side is up. Sprinkle with the brown sugar, and roast for another 5 minutes. This is splendid when served with rich vanilla ice cream. **Serves 2.**

Puffy Dessert Pancake

Once you know how to make this pancake, you can delight your children for breakfast, adding plenty of maple syrup, but there is no reason you can't delight yourself and some friends by serving it for dessert with fresh lemon and powdered sugar. It is most dramatic just out of the oven, and collapses quickly, so serve it right away.

Ingredients
- 1/2 tablespoons (20 g) butter
- 3/4 cup (175 ml) milk
- 3 large eggs
- 2/3 cup (80 g) flour
- 1/4 teaspoon salt
- 1 teaspoon vanilla
- 1 fresh lemon, cut into wedges with seeds removed
- 1/4 cup (25 g) powdered sugar

Preheat the oven to 425°F (220°C, or gas mark 7). Put the butter in an ovenproof skillet. Put the skillet in the oven for 2 to 3 minutes, until the butter is melted. Remove. In a mixing bowl, mix the milk, eggs, flour, salt, and vanilla until just smooth. Pour the batter into the skillet, on top of the melted butter. Place in the oven and bake for 15 minutes, or until puffy and golden. Serve at once with wedges of lemon to squirt on top, and then sprinkle liberally with powdered sugar. **Serves 4.**

Pots de Creme

As we warned you, this is not a dish that emphasizes low calories! But as an occasional indulgence, go for it! And do spend the money on the best chocolate you can find.

Ingredients
- 6 ounces (170 g) high-quality bittersweet chocolate, coarsely chopped
- 1/2 cups (355 ml) whipping cream
- 1/2 cups (355 ml) milk
- 1/4 cup (50 g) sugar
- 8 egg yolks

Preheat the oven to 300°F (150°C, or gas mark 2). Melt the chocolate with ? cup (120 ml) of the cream in a double boiler. Set aside. Combine the remaining 1 cup (235 ml) of cream, milk, and sugar in a saucepan and warm until the sugar seems dissolved. In a separate bowl, whip the egg yolks, and then stir the whipped yolks slowly into the warmed cream. Add the chocolate mixture to this and stir gently. Pour into ramekins or custard cups. Place the cups in a glass baking dish with hot water at least 1 inch (2.5 cm) deep. Bake for 45 minutes. Refrigerate until cold. **Serves 6.**

Beauty and Relaxation

RESOURCES SECTION

Check out these Web sites for MomSpa supplies and products. If you need more help with your search, e-mail us at basyesander@yahoo.com.

Adora spa parties
www.adoraspa.com

DHC Japanese skin care
www.dhccare.com

Drugstore.com (a good source for inexpensive beauty products)
www.drugstore.com

English tea
www.englishteastore.com

Essential oils
www.homespaessentials.com

Glass jars
www.herbalremedies.com

Goldleaf and Hydrangea
www.xanadus.com/the_thymes.asp

Habitat for Humanity
www.habitatforhumanity.org

Herbs
www.oldtimeherbs.com

Juice Plus shakes
www.juiceplus.com

Meditation tapes
www.meditationcenter.com

Tea
www.nicecupofteaandasitdown.com

Nukkles massage tool
www.comfortchannel.com

One Minute Manicure
www.oneminutemanicure.com

Pumpkin peel
(developed by Jeanne Marie)
www.pumpkinpeel.com

Tiffany and Company
(crystal water pitchers)
www.tiffany.com